THE MYSTERY & EXPERIENCE OF PLEASURE

SACHIN J. KARNIK

ISBN: 9798388824479
Imprint: Independently published

Published by:
The Angel Wing, LLC

Distributed by:
Kindle Direct Publications

Additional copies of this book are available at:
Amazon.com and other retailers

Or:
Please get in touch with The Angel Wing, LLC at:
www.TheAngelWing.com
e-mail:theangelwing19@gmail.com

FREE ONLINE PROGRAMS

MONDAY EVENINGS (6 PM TO 7 PM) - MEDITATION WITH DR. CHETANA KRIPALU
WEDNESDAY EVENINGS (7 PM TO 8 PM) – MEDITATION WITH DR. ELIZABETH BERMAN
SUNDAY EVENINGS (7 PM TO 8 PM) – MEDITATIVE DIALOGUE WITH ANGEL WING'S
TUESDAY & THURSDAY EVENINGS (8 PM – 9: 15 PM) - PERSONAL TRANSFORMATION
PROGRAM

PLEASE USE THE LINK AND/OR MEETING ID (WITH PASSWORD) BELOW FOR ALL ONLINE
PROGRAMS:

https://us02web.zoom.us/j/8919816907
Meeting ID: 891 981 6907
Passcode: WqA3u1

DEDICATION

This book is dedicated to all participants in the Angel Wing Program and those interested in unraveling the mysteries of pleasure.

CONTENTS

ACKNOWLEDGEMENTS
7

PREFACE
9

CONCEPT OF PLEASURE
15

SCIENCE OF PLEASURE
23

PHILOSOPHY OF PLEASURE
43

CULTURAL PERSPECTIVE OF PLEASURE
51

DARK SIDE OF PLEASURE
79

SPIRITUAL DIMENSION OF PLEASURE
89

ART OF PLEASURE
97

REFERENCES
105

ABOUT THE AUTHOR
121

ACKNOWLEDGMENTS

The author would like to give special acknowledgment to Dr. Chetana Kripalu and Dr. Elizabeth Berman for their continued guidance and encouragement in studying and contemplating many aspects of the human condition.

PREFACE

Greetings and welcome to Angel Wing, LLC. We are pleased to present our latest publication, crafted with good research conducted by Sachin Karnik. Sachin's efforts have been commendable and noteworthy, and we are grateful for his contribution. It is important to note that Sachin Karnik is the first participant of Angel Wing's Quantum Transformation Program (QTP), designed to facilitate personal transformation and growth. Sachin's dedication to his development, as well as to the development of Angel Wing, has been exemplary. His contributions have been invaluable in shaping our approach toward achieving our goals.

Angel Wing is dedicated to creating a positive impact on the world by facilitating personal and collective transformation. We are committed to building a safe, supportive environment fostering growth and learning. Our approach can help individuals overcome personal challenges and achieve their goals using systematic methods. The Quantum Transformation Program is designed to provide individuals with the tools, resources, and support they need to reach their full potential.

We are proud of our team and their contributions toward our vision of creating a world where everyone can achieve their full potential. We are committed to continuing our research and development efforts to ensure we remain at the forefront of personal transformation. We look forward to welcoming more participants into our Quantum Transformation Program and continuing to impact the world positively.

At the foundation of the Angel Wing, LLC lies a set of three guiding principles we hold in high regard. These principles form the basis of our philosophy and approach to positively impacting the world. The guiding principles of Angel Wing are self-mastery, personal transformation, and human upliftment, each of which is essential to achieving our vision.

<u>Self-mastery</u> is the first guiding principle of Angel Wing. We believe that individuals must control their emotions, thoughts, and behaviors to achieve personal growth and development. Self-mastery involves developing self-awareness and self-discipline, critical skills for success in any endeavor. We encourage our participants to focus on self-mastery to achieve their full potential and lead fulfilling lives.

The second guiding principle of Angel Wing is <u>personal transformation</u>. We believe that personal transformation is a necessary aspect of growth and development.

Personal transformation involves a fundamental shift in one's values, beliefs, and behaviors, leading to a profound change in one's life. We support our participants in their personal transformation journeys, providing them with the resources and guidance they need to make lasting changes.

The third guiding principle of Angel Wing is <u>human upliftment</u>. Human upliftment involves addressing social inequalities and promoting individual growth and development. We believe our responsibility is to create a more just and equitable society. We are committed to supporting our participants in their efforts to positively impact the world through their actions or contributions to the community.

The guiding principles of Angel Wing, LLC are self-mastery, personal transformation, and human upliftment. These principles form the foundation of our philosophy and approach to positively impacting the world. Understanding these principles is critical to achieving personal growth and development and positively impacting the world. We believe that by focusing on these principles, we can help individuals reach their full potential and make a meaningful contribution to society. Provided below is a brief overview of each of our guiding principles.

<u>SELF-MASTERY</u>

Self-mastery is the ability to control one's emotions, thoughts, and behaviors. It is the capacity to regulate one's reactions and impulses to align with one's values and goals. Developing self-mastery requires a great deal of self-awareness, self-reflection, and self-discipline. It is an ongoing process that involves continuous learning and growth. One of the benefits of self-mastery is the ability to make better decisions. When individuals have control over their emotions, they are less likely to make impulsive decisions that may have negative consequences. Instead, they can take a step back and evaluate the situation objectively, considering the potential outcomes of their actions. This allows individuals to make decisions more aligned with their values and goals. Self-mastery can also improve one's relationships with others. When individuals control their emotions, they are less likely to act out in ways that may harm others. They can communicate effectively, empathize with others, and maintain healthy boundaries. This can lead to more robust and more fulfilling relationships with friends, family, and colleagues. Self-mastery is an important skill to develop to lead a fulfilling and successful life. It requires self-awareness, self-reflection, and self-discipline. The benefits of self-mastery are numerous, including better decision-making and stronger relationships with others. Individuals can achieve greater success and happiness in their personal and professional lives by focusing on developing self-mastery.

PERSONAL TRANSFORMATION

Personal transformation refers to a profound change within an individual, leading to a fundamental shift in their values, beliefs, and behaviors. It is a process of personal growth that involves moving from one state of being to another, often in response to a significant life event or a desire for self-improvement. Personal transformation is a journey that requires self-reflection, self-awareness, and a willingness to change. The process of personal transformation can be challenging, as it often requires individuals to confront their fears, limiting beliefs, and negative thought patterns. It can involve letting go of old habits and ways of thinking and embracing new perspectives and practices of being. Personal transformation is not a one-time event but an ongoing process involving continuous learning and growth. The benefits of personal transformation are numerous. It can lead to greater self-awareness, improved relationships with others, increased resilience, and a sense of purpose and meaning in life. Personal transformation can also improve physical and mental health as individuals learn to manage their emotions and prioritize self-care. There are many ways to facilitate personal transformation, including therapy, self-help books, workshops, and retreats. These tools can provide individuals with the knowledge, skills, and support they need to navigate the process of personal transformation. However, the most crucial factor in personal transformation is the individual's willingness to change and commitment to the process. Personal transformation is a journey of self-discovery and growth that involves a fundamental shift in values, beliefs, and behaviors. It can be a challenging process, but the numerous benefits include greater self-awareness, improved relationships, increased resilience, and a sense of purpose and meaning in life. Personal transformation is an ongoing process that requires a commitment to self-reflection, learning, and growth and can be facilitated through various tools and resources. Personal transformation is a journey towards a more fulfilling and meaningful life.

HUMAN UPLIFTMENT

The process of human upliftment refers to the ongoing effort to improve humanity's physical, social, emotional, and spiritual well-being. It is a multifaceted process that addresses systemic inequalities and promotes individual growth and development. Human upliftment is a collective effort that requires collaboration and innovation. Angel Wing promotes these ideals by encouraging each individual to engage in a systematic process of personal transformation. As more people engage in this process, human upliftment will occur naturally. Another aspect of human upliftment is promoting education and skill development. Education is critical to individual growth and development and can lead to more significant economic opportunities and social mobility. Promoting education may involve increasing access to quality schools and training programs and supporting individuals to pursue higher education and training. Angel Wing provides many online educational programs for the development of each person. A significant aspect of human upliftment is promoting personal growth and development. This involves providing individuals with the tools, resources, and support they need to develop their full potential. Efforts to promote personal growth and development may include providing access to counseling and mental health services, promoting healthy lifestyle choices, and supporting individuals to pursue their passions and interests. Human upliftment also involves fostering spiritual growth and development. This provides individuals with the space and resources to explore their spiritual beliefs and practices. Promoting spiritual growth and development may include supporting religious and spiritual communities, promoting mindfulness and meditation practices, and providing access to spiritual counseling and guidance. The process of human upliftment is an ongoing effort to improve humanity's physical, social, emotional, and spiritual well-being. This multifaceted process involves addressing basic needs, promoting education and skill development, addressing social inequalities, promoting personal growth and development, and promoting spiritual growth and development. Efforts to uplift humanity require a collective commitment to social justice, innovation, and collaboration.

BRIEF REFLECTIONS ON PLEASURE

With this overview of Angel Wing's vision, Angel Wing has multiple areas, including publication. Along these lines, the Angel Wing Quantum Transformation Program has started extensive research on the problem of addiction. The current publication is an attempt to introduce, in a general sense, the phenomenon of pleasure. An introductory overview of the nature of pleasure and its many aspects will serve as a gateway into more specific publications about the role of pleasure in addictions. Also, given that the current publication introduces pleasure, I would like to share my thoughts about this subject.

Each human being experiences pleasure in many different ways, and the source of pleasure varies from person to person. The factors contributing to pleasure are multifaceted and can be influenced by various individual, environmental, and situational factors. However, one commonality among all humans is the desire to seek pleasure and avoid pain. For some people, pleasure may come from achievement or accomplishment. These individuals derive pleasure from completing tasks or reaching goals that they have set for themselves. This can be as simple as finishing a household chore or as complex as achieving a significant milestone in their career. The sense of satisfaction that comes from these accomplishments can create feelings of pleasure and fulfillment. For others, pleasure may come from socializing and spending time with loved ones. Humans are social creatures, and we derive pleasure from interacting with others. Engaging in dinners, parties, or simply spending time with friends and family can create happiness and joy. Some enjoy engaging in creative pursuits, such as writing, painting, or playing music. These activities can generate a sense of flow, where individuals lose track of time and become fully immersed in their creative endeavors. The sense of accomplishment and pride that results from creating something unique can create feelings of pleasure and satisfaction. For some people, pursuing pleasure may be linked to their physical well-being. Exercise and physical activity can release endorphins, which are hormones that promote feelings of joy and happiness.

For many people, pleasure is linked to relaxation and calmness. Similarly, consuming certain foods, such as chocolate or spicy foods, can activate the brain's pleasure centers and create euphoria. Engaging in activities such as reading, attending lectures, or learning a new skill can create a sense of pleasure and satisfaction. Engaging in meditation, yoga, or mindfulness activities can help reduce stress levels and promote a sense of well-being. Similarly, spending time in nature or engaging in outdoor activities such as hiking or camping can also promote feelings of pleasure and relaxation. Satisfaction can also be linked to the pursuit of knowledge and intellectual growth. For many people, pursuing knowledge is essential to personal growth and can lead to feelings of fulfillment and happiness. However, it is crucial to note that pleasure-seeking can also lead to negative consequences. Individuals may engage in substance abuse or risky sexual behavior to pursue pleasure, which can adversely affect their physical and mental health. Therefore, balancing seeking pleasure and engaging in behaviors that promote overall well-being is essential. Each human being experiences pleasure in many different ways and the factors contributing to pleasure are multifaceted. Whether through achievement, socialization, creativity, physical activity, relaxation, or the pursuit of knowledge, seeking pleasure is a fundamental aspect of human nature. However, engaging in behaviors that promote overall well-being and strive for a balance between pleasure-seeking and self-care is essential.

In closing, I would like to express my appreciation to Sachin Karnik for taking the time to research this subject and present it straightforwardly. I would also like to encourage all readers to participate in Angel Wing online programming. These programs, generously offered at no cost to the public, aim to foster a deep understanding and appreciation of the three guiding principles that form the foundation of the Angel Wing initiative: self-mastery, personal transformation, and human upliftment. By making these programs accessible to all, the organizers hope to inspire a diverse range of participants to embark on a journey of self-discovery and growth, empowering them to reach their full potential and ultimately contribute to the betterment of society.

As participants in the Angel Wing programs, individuals are encouraged to explore and embrace the concepts of self-mastery, which entails developing discipline, self-awareness, and emotional intelligence. This self-mastery then paves the way for personal transformation, allowing individuals to overcome limiting beliefs, habits, and thought patterns that may have held them back in the past. Through this transformative process, participants are guided towards a path of human upliftment, where they can positively impact the lives of others by sharing their insights, experiences, and newfound wisdom. The Angel Wing programs serve as a platform for personal growth and collective change, fostering a sense of community and mutual support among all those who share an interest in self-improvement and the betterment of the world around them.

Chetana Kripalu, MD
Founder/CEO
The Angel Wing, LLC

CONCEPT OF PLEASURE

Pleasure, as a multidimensional construct, has been a focal point of philosophical, psychological, and neuroscientific exploration for centuries. The hedonic experience of pleasure is generally typified by positive affective states and sensations of enjoyment, gratification, and reward. This experience can emerge from an array of activities, such as consuming food, engaging in sexual experiences, and participating in social interactions. Neurotransmitters and other biochemical factors in the brain, including dopamine and endorphins, modulate pleasure (Berridge, 2003). The import of pleasure in human existence is profound, serving as a fundamental human necessity that contributes to overall well-being and life quality (Diener et al., 2017). Empirical evidence demonstrates that pleasurable experiences can bolster positive emotions, alleviate stress, and promote improved mental health outcomes, such as diminished anxiety and depression (Kashdan et al., 2008). Furthermore, pleasure has been correlated with enhanced cognitive function, including heightened creativity and productivity (Hansen et al., 2015). Nonetheless, pleasure-seeking may present potential disadvantages. While typically perceived as an adaptive facet of human behavior, it can occasionally result in negative repercussions, such as addiction and social isolation (Twenge et al., 2020). The hedonic pursuit of pleasure may be subject to cultural and social influences and may vary based on individual disparities in personality and situational contexts. Thus, it is crucial to fathom the intricate nature of pleasure and its potential implications for human behavior and well-being. A comprehensive understanding of pleasure necessitates rigorous examination from multiple disciplines. As a complex and nuanced construct, pleasure encompasses psychological and physiological benefits. However, its pursuit can also entail potential drawbacks, with individual and contextual factors playing a role. This underscores the importance of grasping the elaborate nature of pleasure and its potential consequences for human behavior and well-being.[0.1]

THE HEDONIC EXPERIENCE OF PLEASURE

The notion of pleasure can be conceptualized as a positive sensation or emotion elicited by specific experiences or activities. Manifesting in various forms, such as physical phenomena, emotional states, or cognitive processes, pleasure is often juxtaposed with pain or discomfort and is typically linked to happiness, enjoyment, or satisfaction. The hedonic theory of pleasure posits that pleasure serves as the ultimate objective of human behavior, suggesting that individuals are motivated to pursue pleasure while avoiding pain. This theory implies that all human actions are fundamentally driven by the desire to optimize pleasure and minimize pain. In terms of brain function, pleasure is connected to the release of specific neurotransmitters, such as dopamine, which play a crucial role in mood and motivation regulation. The experience of pleasure is also influenced by an array of environmental and individual factors, including social context, cultural norms, and personal inclinations.

The hedonic experience of pleasure, characterized by positive emotions like joy, satisfaction, and reward, is modulated by multiple neurochemical factors within the brain. Dopamine, one of the primary neurotransmitters involved in the modulation of pleasure, is released in response to pleasurable stimuli and is implicated in the brain's reward system (Kringelbach, 2005). Dopamine release in the nucleus accumbens—a brain region associated with reward processing—has been linked to the experience of pleasure resulting from various stimuli, such as food and substances of abuse (Berridge & Kringelbach, 2015). Endorphins, another neurochemical component of the hedonic pleasure experience, are endogenous opioid peptides released in response to diverse stimuli, including physical exercise and social interactions (Zagon & McLaughlin, 2014). Binding to opioid receptors in the brain, endorphins produce analgesic and euphoric effects associated with the experience of pleasure.

Moreover, the hedonic experience of pleasure is not exclusively dependent on the release of neurotransmitters and other biochemical factors in the brain. Psychological and social factors, such as expectations, cultural norms, and social contexts, also influence the experience of pleasure (Mikulincer & Shaver, 2016). For instance, cultural norms and social expectations may shape the pleasure derived from eating, while the nature of interpersonal relationships may affect the pleasure resulting from social interactions. The hedonic experience of pleasure thus constitutes a complex phenomenon modulated by several neurochemical factors, including dopamine and endorphins. While the release of these neurochemicals in response to pleasurable stimuli is associated with pleasure, psychological and social factors also contribute to the experience, underscoring the intricate and multifaceted nature of pleasure.[1.1]

THE IMPORTANCE OF EXPLORING
THE MYSTERY OF PLEASURE

Investigating the enigma of pleasure is crucial for multiple reasons. First, pleasure constitutes a fundamental component of the human experience, substantially impacting physical and mental well-being as well as social and interpersonal relationships. Comprehending the nature of pleasure and how it contributes to happier, healthier lives is invaluable. Second, pleasure presents as a complex, multifaceted phenomenon that has been the focus of extensive scientific research and philosophical discourse. Delving into the mystery of pleasure facilitates a deeper understanding of its underlying mechanisms, relationships with other psychological processes, and the role it plays in shaping human behavior and culture. The study of pleasure bears significant implications for various fields, including psychology, neuroscience, philosophy, and sociology. Advancing our knowledge of pleasure enables professionals to develop more effective treatments for psychological disorders, enhance our understanding of addiction and compulsive behaviors, and gain insights into human motivation and decision-making. Pleasure is an essential human experience that is integral to physical and mental well-being. Participating in pleasurable activities such as spending time with loved ones, listening to music, or savoring a delicious meal can promote happiness, relaxation, and fulfillment. Pleasure can also yield numerous physical health benefits, such as reducing stress and anxiety levels, fostering better sleep quality, and fortifying the immune system (Pressman & Cohen, 2005). Thus, incorporating pleasurable activities into daily routines can help individuals achieve optimal health and well-being. Furthermore, pleasure can influence social and interpersonal relationships. Engaging in enjoyable activities with others, like attending concerts or sharing meals, can reinforce social bonds and foster feelings of connection and belonging. Pleasure can also enhance intimacy and sustain romantic relationships. Research indicates that engaging in pleasurable activities with a partner, such as sexual activity or romantic getaways, can intensify feelings of love and attachment (Aron et al., 2000). Therefore, pleasure is beneficial for well-being and significantly affects social and interpersonal relationships. Nonetheless, it is essential to acknowledge that the pursuit of pleasure can also yield negative consequences. Indulging excessively or unhealthily in pleasurable activities, such as substance abuse or overeating, can result in addiction, health issues, and other detrimental outcomes (Blum et al., 2000). Consequently, seeking balance and moderation in the pursuit of pleasure and engaging in activities that bolster physical and mental well-being while supporting social relationships is of paramount importance.[2.1]

PHYSICAL AND MENTAL WELL-BEING

Comprehending the nature of pleasure and its functionality can profoundly influence our physical and mental well-being as well as social and interpersonal relationships. For instance, research demonstrates that experiencing positive emotions, encompassing pleasure, can yield a multitude of physical health benefits, including reduced inflammation, decreased blood pressure, and enhanced immune system function (Fredrickson, 2001; Pressman & Cohen, 2005). Moreover, the pursuit of pleasure can propel individuals to adopt healthy behaviors, such as exercising, consuming nutritious foods, and ensuring sufficient sleep, which can further ameliorate health outcomes (Patrick et al., 2013). Understanding the nature of pleasure holds critical implications for mental health and well-being as well. For example, pleasure can furnish a sense of reward and fulfillment, fostering positive self-esteem, self-worth, and overall life satisfaction (Ryan & Deci, 2001). Furthermore, discerning the factors that influence pleasure can enable individuals to make informed decisions about the activities and experiences they pursue. This awareness can help promote positive emotions and mitigate the risk of adverse outcomes, such as addiction or harmful behaviors (Duhigg, 2012). Comprehending the nature of pleasure bears significant implications for social and interpersonal relationships too. Pleasure is frequently experienced in social interactions, and understanding its role in social behavior can assist individuals in cultivating more resilient and meaningful connections with others (Riggio & Throckmorton, 2001). For example, sharing pleasurable experiences with others can facilitate feelings of closeness, trust, and intimacy, which can positively impact social relationships and overall well-being (Gable et al., 2004).[2.2]

<u>PLEASURE IS A COMPLEX AND MULTIFACETED PHENOMENON</u>

Pleasure is a complex and multidimensional phenomenon that has been the focus of extensive scientific research and philosophical inquiry. From a scientific perspective, understanding the neural mechanisms underpinning pleasure and reward can elucidate how these processes shape behavior and influence decision-making. For example, dopamine release in response to pleasurable stimuli has been connected to various behaviors, including drug addiction and compulsive gambling (Kringelbach & Berridge, 2010). Furthermore, research has demonstrated that the experience of pleasure can be modulated by a range of individual and contextual factors, such as genetics, culture, and social norms (Knobloch-Westerwick & Meng, 2009). This suggests that pleasure is a highly intricate phenomenon shaped by a wide array of interacting factors. Philosophical inquiry into pleasure has also significantly impacted our understanding of this phenomenon. From ancient Greek philosophers like Epicurus and Aristotle to contemporary thinkers like Martha Nussbaum and Susan Wolf, philosophers have explored the nature of pleasure and its relationship to happiness, well-being, and morality (Nussbaum, 1990; Wolf, 2010). For instance, some philosophers have posited that pleasure is essential for a good life, while others have emphasized the perils of hedonism and the need to balance pleasure with other values, such as virtue and meaning. Philosophical debates surrounding pleasure persist in shaping our comprehension of this complex and multifaceted phenomenon. Understanding the nature of pleasure bears significant implications for our well-being and quality of life. Research has revealed that the experience of pleasure can yield positive effects on physical and mental health, encompassing reduced stress levels, improved mood, and heightened social connectedness (Kringelbach & Berridge, 2010; Pressman & Cohen, 2005). Moreover, interventions promoting pleasure, like engaging in hobbies, spending time with loved ones, or practicing mindfulness, have been shown to effectively enhance well-being and alleviate symptoms of anxiety and depression (Chida & Steptoe, 2008; Garland et al., 2015). By deepening our understanding of the nature of pleasure and its operation, we can devise strategies to foster pleasure and well-being in our lives and society at large.[2.3]

UNDERLYING MECHANISMS – SHAPING BEHAVIOR & CULTURE

The study of pleasure has captivated scientists and philosophers for centuries and persists as a subject of ongoing research and inquiry. By scrutinizing pleasure's intricate and multifaceted nature, researchers can attain insights into the underlying biological, psychological, and social mechanisms that mold our pleasure experiences. This knowledge can inform the development of interventions that foster positive pleasure experiences while mitigating the adverse consequences of excessive or detrimental pleasure-seeking behaviors. One area of research illuminating the mechanisms underpinning pleasure involves examining the brain's reward system. This system encompasses the release of neurotransmitters like dopamine and endorphins, which are associated with sensations of pleasure, euphoria, and reward. The release of these chemicals is believed to be triggered by various stimuli, such as food, sex, drugs, and social interactions. Understanding this system's functioning can inform interventions aimed at managing addictive behaviors and encouraging healthy pleasure-seeking behaviors. Additionally, researchers have investigated the relationship between pleasure and other psychological processes, including motivation, emotion, and cognition. For instance, pleasure is often regarded as a crucial motivator of behavior, with individuals driven by the pursuit of pleasure and the avoidance of pain. Moreover, pleasure can influence our emotional experiences, such as enhancing positive affect and diminishing negative affect. By examining the complex interplay between pleasure and these other psychological processes, researchers can acquire a more nuanced comprehension of the role that pleasure serves in shaping human behavior and experience.[2.4]

IMPLICATIONS FOR A RANGE OF FIELDS

The study of pleasure encompasses a multidisciplinary field with significant implications for various scientific and philosophical domains. Discerning the mechanisms underlying pleasure in psychology and neuroscience can facilitate our comprehension of how motivation and reward systems operate within the brain

(Kringelbach & Berridge, 2010). This understanding can be applied to develop interventions aimed at treating addiction, depression, and other mental health conditions involving disruptions in reward processing (Berridge, 2007). In philosophy, the study of pleasure has garnered interest for millennia, with thinkers such as Epicurus and Aristotle proposing distinct theories of what constitutes a pleasurable life. Contemporary philosophers persist in exploring the nature of pleasure and its relationship with other aspects of human experiences, such as meaning and happiness (Haybron, 2008). In sociology, investigating pleasure can illuminate how cultural norms and values shape individuals' pleasure experiences and influence social behavior (Gill & Orgad, 2017). Furthermore, the study of pleasure can also have practical applications in fields like marketing and design. Understanding the factors contributing to pleasurable experiences can inform the development of products and services catering to consumer needs and preferences (Hirschman & Holbrook, 1982). Additionally, a more profound understanding of pleasure and its role in human behavior can inform interventions to promote health and well-being, such as encouraging healthy eating, exercise, and social interaction (Kahneman et al., 1999).[2.5]

IMPLICATIONS FOR DEVELOPING EFFECTIVE TREATMENTS

Understanding the intricate nature of pleasure carries significant implications for developing effective treatments for psychological disorders. For instance, research indicates that the brain's reward and pleasure centers are dysregulated in addiction, depression, and other disorders, suggesting that therapies targeting these mechanisms may effectively treat these conditions (Nestler & Carlezon, 2006; Volkow et al., 2010). Furthermore, interventions that promote positive affect and pleasurable experiences have been shown to effectively reduce symptoms of depression and anxiety (Fava & Tomba, 2010). In addition to enhancing our understanding of psychological disorders, studying pleasure can provide insights into addiction and other compulsive behaviors. The experience of pleasure is considered to play a vital role in addiction, with repeated exposure to pleasurable stimuli leading to alterations in the brain's reward and motivation systems that promote compulsive drug-seeking behaviors (Koob & Volkow, 2016). By attaining a deeper understanding of the underlying mechanisms of addiction and other compulsive behaviors, professionals can develop more effective interventions for these conditions. Exploring the nature of pleasure can offer insights into human motivation and decision-making. For example, theories of motivation often incorporate pleasure as a critical factor in driving behavior, with some suggesting that individuals are primarily motivated by the pursuit of pleasure and the avoidance of pain (Fishbein & Ajzen, 2010). Moreover, research has demonstrated that the experience of pleasure can influence a wide range of cognitive processes, including attention, memory, and decision-making (Berridge, 2009). By better understanding how pleasure operates within these processes, researchers can develop more accurate models of human behavior and decision-making.[2.6]

<u>Reflective Questions:</u>

1. How do your personal beliefs, values, and cultural background influence your understanding and pursuit of pleasure? In what ways do these factors shape the types of experiences you find pleasurable?

2. How has your perception of pleasure evolved over time, and what experiences or insights have contributed to this evolution? Can you identify any specific moments or events that led to a shift in your understanding of pleasure?

3. In what ways can the pursuit of pleasure contribute to personal growth and self-discovery? Conversely, are there potential drawbacks or challenges associated with placing a strong emphasis on seeking pleasure in one's life?

4. How do societal norms and expectations influence our understanding and pursuit of pleasure? What role does societal pressure play in shaping our individual and collective perceptions of what is considered pleasurable?

5. How can an increased awareness of the neurobiological and psychological underpinnings of pleasure inform our approach to seeking and cultivating pleasurable experiences in our lives? How might this knowledge help us achieve a more balanced and fulfilling life?

SCIENCE OF PLEASURE

THE ROLE OF THE BRAIN IN PLEASURE

The brain is central to the experience of pleasure, which is a complex phenomenon involving the activation of a network of brain regions, including the prefrontal cortex, limbic system, basal ganglia, and other areas. The prefrontal cortex is responsible for the cognitive and emotional aspects of pleasure, such as anticipating and evaluating rewarding stimuli. The limbic system, encompassing the nucleus accumbens, amygdala, and hippocampus, plays a role in processing emotional and motivational aspects of pleasure. The basal ganglia, particularly the ventral striatum, are involved in processing the hedonic aspects of pleasure, including the subjective feeling of pleasure or reward. Research has demonstrated that the brain's pleasure circuitry is implicated in various behaviors, including eating, drinking, socializing, sex, and drug use. Dysregulation of this circuitry can result in addiction, depression, and other psychiatric disorders.[3]

1. The brain plays an essential role in experiencing pleasure, a complex phenomenon that requires the activation of numerous brain regions, including the prefrontal cortex, limbic system, basal ganglia, among others (Kringelbach & Berridge, 2009). Gaining insight into the neural foundations of pleasure is vital for elucidating the underlying mechanisms of human behavior and creating therapeutic interventions for psychiatric disorders associated with disturbances in pleasure processing.[3.12]

2. The prefrontal cortex (PFC) is responsible for the cognitive and emotional aspects of pleasure, such as anticipating and evaluating rewarding stimuli (Kringelbach, 2005). This region of the brain is involved in higher-order cognitive functions, including decision-making, planning, and the regulation of emotions. Research has shown that the PFC's activity during pleasurable experiences can modulate the subjective feelings of pleasure and influence the motivation to pursue rewarding stimuli (Kringelbach & Rolls, 2004).[3.12]

3. The limbic system, which includes the nucleus accumbens, amygdala, and hippocampus, plays a crucial role in processing emotional and motivational aspects of pleasure (Berridge & Kringelbach, 2015). The nucleus accumbens, a key component of the brain's reward system, is responsible for the release of dopamine, a neurotransmitter associated with pleasure and motivation (Schultz, 2016). The nucleus accumbens' activation is critical for the reinforcement of behaviors and the formation of associations between

pleasurable stimuli and their outcomes (Nestler, 2005).[3.12]

4. The amygdala, another component of the limbic system, is involved in processing emotional aspects of pleasure, particularly the affective evaluation of rewarding stimuli (Baxter & Murray, 2002). This almond-shaped structure is essential for encoding the emotional valence of stimuli, which can influence motivation and decision-making processes. The amygdala's activation during pleasurable experiences can modulate the intensity of subjective feelings of pleasure and contribute to the formation of emotional memories related to rewarding events (Pessoa & Adolphs, 2010).[3.12]

5. The hippocampus, also part of the limbic system, plays a role in processing the contextual aspects of pleasure experiences (Lisman & Grace, 2005). This brain region is critical for the formation and retrieval of episodic memories, which can include information about the spatial, temporal, and situational aspects of pleasurable events. The hippocampus' involvement in pleasure processing can contribute to the formation of associations between rewarding stimuli and their contexts, which can in turn influence future motivation and decision-making (Eichenbaum, 2017).[3.12]

6. The basal ganglia, particularly the ventral striatum, are involved in processing the hedonic aspects of pleasure, including the subjective feeling of pleasure or reward (Berridge et al., 2009). The ventral striatum's activation during pleasurable experiences is associated with the release of endogenous opioids, neurotransmitters that contribute to the subjective feeling of pleasure and the reinforcement of rewarding behaviors (Fields, 2007).[3.12]

7. Research has demonstrated that the brain's pleasure circuitry is implicated in various behaviors, including eating, drinking, socializing, sex, and drug use (Kringelbach & Berridge, 2009). The activation of these brain regions in response to pleasurable stimuli can promote the pursuit of rewarding experiences and contribute to the formation of habits and preferences (Everitt & Robbins, 2005).[3.12]

8. Dysregulation of the brain's pleasure circuitry can result in addiction, depression, and other psychiatric disorders (Nestler & Carlezon, 2006; Volkow et al., 2010). For example, addiction has been linked to alterations in the functioning of the brain's reward system, including changes in dopamine transmission and receptor availability (Koob & Volkow, 2016). These neurobiological changes can result in a decreased sensitivity to natural rewards

and an increased craving for drugs or other addictive substances. Understanding the neural mechanisms underlying addiction can inform the development of targeted interventions for the prevention and treatment of substance use disorders (Volkow & Morales, 2015).[3.12]

9. Depression has been associated with disruptions in the brain's pleasure circuitry, including reduced activity in the nucleus accumbens and the prefrontal cortex (Pizzagalli, 2014). These alterations in neural functioning can lead to anhedonia, a core symptom of depression characterized by a reduced capacity to experience pleasure (Treadway & Zald, 2011). Developing a deeper understanding of the neural basis of pleasure and its dysregulation in depression can inform the development of novel treatments, such as pharmacological interventions targeting the brain's reward system, or cognitive-behavioral therapies aimed at enhancing the experience of pleasure in daily activities (Rizvi et al., 2016).[3.12]

10. The study of the brain's pleasure circuitry can also contribute to our understanding of other psychiatric disorders characterized by alterations in reward processing, such as bipolar disorder and schizophrenia (Whitton et al., 2015). For instance, individuals with bipolar disorder often exhibit heightened reward sensitivity during manic episodes, which can result in impulsive and risky behaviors (Mason et al., 2012). On the other hand, individuals with schizophrenia may exhibit reduced hedonic capacity, contributing to negative symptoms such as anhedonia and social withdrawal (Gard et al., 2007). Investigating the neural underpinnings of pleasure in these disorders can inform the development of targeted interventions aimed at restoring the balance in reward processing and enhancing overall well-being (Whitton et al., 2015).[3.12]

11. In addition to its implications for mental health, the study of pleasure and its neural correlates can also inform our understanding of individual differences in the experience of pleasure. For example, genetic factors have been found to influence the functioning of the brain's dopamine system, contributing to variations in reward sensitivity and the propensity for engaging in pleasure-seeking behaviors (Bogdan et al., 2016). Understanding the genetic basis of individual differences in pleasure can provide insights into the development of personalized interventions to promote well-being and prevent maladaptive behaviors (Bogdan et al., 2016).[3.12]

PLEASURE & THE BRAIN

Pleasure, as a multifaceted and intricate phenomenon, relies on the activation of various brain regions responsible for processing sensory information and emotional states (Berridge & Kringelbach, 2015). Gaining insight into the brain's role in pleasure processing is essential for understanding human behavior and developing targeted interventions for psychiatric disorders. The prefrontal cortex, a crucial part of the pleasure network, is responsible for the cognitive and emotional aspects of pleasure, including anticipation, evaluation, and decision-making related to rewarding stimuli (Kringelbach, 2018). This region allows us to comprehend the context of pleasurable experiences, facilitating informed choices about participating in activities that optimize pleasure while minimizing potential harm. The limbic system, comprising the nucleus accumbens, amygdala, and hippocampus, plays a critical role in processing emotional and motivational aspects of pleasure (Berridge & Kringelbach, 2015). The nucleus accumbens, a key component of the brain's reward system, integrates information from various brain regions and modulates dopamine release, a neurotransmitter associated with pleasure and reward (Volkow et al., 2011). The amygdala processes emotional aspects of pleasurable experiences, while the hippocampus contributes to memory formation and consolidation, allowing us to recall and learn from past pleasurable experiences. The basal ganglia, particularly the ventral striatum, are essential regions involved in processing hedonic aspects of pleasure, such as the subjective feeling of pleasure or reward (Kringelbach & Berridge, 2009). This area collaborates with the limbic system and prefrontal cortex, forming a neural circuit that reinforces rewarding behaviors and guides our choices based on previous pleasurable experiences. Research underscores the importance of the brain's pleasure circuitry in a variety of behaviors, including eating, drinking, socializing, sex, and drug use (Kringelbach, 2018). Dysregulation in the function of these brain regions or imbalances in neurotransmitter systems, such as dopamine, can result in psychiatric disorders like addiction and depression (Volkow et al., 2010). Consequently, elucidating the neural basis of pleasure processing is vital for developing targeted interventions and therapies aimed at promoting mental health and well-being.

The prefrontal cortex is involved in cognitive and executive functions, such as decision-making and attentional control, while the limbic system plays a role in emotional regulation and processing reward-related stimuli. The basal ganglia, on the other hand, regulate movement and motivation. Research indicates that pleasure experiences are associated with neurotransmitters, like dopamine, which are crucial to the brain's reward and motivation systems (Berridge & Kringelbach, 2015). The release of dopamine in response to pleasurable stimuli can reinforce behaviors leading to pleasure, potentially resulting in habits or addictions. For instance, repeated dopamine release due to drug use can cause addiction and compulsive drug-seeking behavior (Volkow & Koob, 2015). Individual differences, such as genetics, personality traits, and cultural background, can influence the experience of pleasure (Knobloch-Westerwick & Meng, 2009). Certain genetic variations may affect the intensity of pleasure experienced in response to specific stimuli, like food or drugs (Comings et al., 1999). Similarly, cultural norms and expectations can shape how individuals experience pleasure and determine which types are acceptable or desirable (Burr & Barman-Adhikari, 2019). The study of pleasure and its underlying mechanisms holds significant implications for understanding human behavior and developing interventions to promote health and well-being. Research reveals that different pleasure types activate distinct neural circuits in the brain. Social pleasures, such as praise or social interactions, activate brain regions related to social cognition and emotion regulation. In contrast, sensory pleasures, like eating delicious food or listening to music, involve brain areas associated with sensory processing and reward (Kringelbach, 2019). Understanding the neural basis of pleasure is crucial for developing interventions to address pleasure-related disorders, such as addiction and depression. Addiction, for instance, is thought to involve dysregulation of the brain's reward system, potentially leading to compulsive drug-seeking behavior (Koob & Volkow, 2016). By comprehending how different pleasure types activate distinct neural circuits, researchers can develop targeted interventions to restore balance to the reward system and reduce addiction risk. Additionally, the study of pleasure has broader societal implications, as research on its neural basis can inform public policy decisions related to drug regulation and help us better understand the impact of social policies on pleasure and well-being (Berridge, 2017). Studying the neural correlates of pleasure offers valuable insights into the complex mechanisms underlying this phenomenon, including motivation, reward, and emotion interplay. By understanding the neural basis of pleasure, researchers and clinicians can develop more effective interventions to treat disorders related to pleasure and motivation, such as addiction and depression.

THE PREFRONTAL CORTEX & PLEASURE

The prefrontal cortex is a critical brain region involved in pleasure's cognitive and emotional aspects, such as anticipating and evaluating rewarding stimuli. Studies have shown that the prefrontal cortex is activated when anticipating pleasurable experiences, such as the sight or smell of food. This activation is linked to subjective feelings of desire and motivation (Kringelbach et al., 2012). Additionally, research has suggested that the prefrontal cortex is involved in evaluating pleasurable experiences, such as the taste of food or the feeling of social connection. This evaluation is crucial in determining the intensity and duration of the pleasure experienced (Rolls, 2016). Furthermore, the prefrontal cortex is also involved in regulating and controlling the experience of pleasure. For example, studies have shown that individuals with damage to the prefrontal cortex may experience heightened pleasure and have difficulty controlling their impulses, leading to behaviors such as overeating or drug use (Bechara, 2005). Additionally, research has suggested that the prefrontal cortex plays a role in decision-making related to pleasurable experiences, such as weighing the potential risks and rewards of engaging in certain behaviors (Bickel et al., 2007). The prefrontal cortex is critical in pleasure's cognitive and emotional aspects. Understanding the function and mechanisms of this brain region can provide valuable insights into how pleasure is experienced and regulated in the human brain.[3.2]

THE LIMBIC SYSTEM & PLEASURE

The limbic system, comprising the nucleus accumbens, amygdala, and hippocampus, is integral to the emotional and motivational aspects of pleasure (Berridge & Kringelbach, 2015). This complex network of brain structures plays various roles, including emotion, motivation, learning, and memory, significantly influencing the human experience of pleasure. The nucleus accumbens, often referred to as the "pleasure center" of the brain, is activated by rewarding stimuli, such as food, drugs, and social interactions (Wise, 2004). Research has demonstrated that nucleus accumbens activation correlates with increased dopamine release, a critical factor in experiencing pleasure (Schultz, 2015). The amygdala, another essential limbic system structure, contributes to the emotional processing of pleasure and is thought to be involved in forming positive emotional memories (Phelps, 2004). For instance, studies have found that the sight or smell of food activates the amygdala, with this activation being associated with pleasure experiences (Rolls, 2005). Moreover, the hippocampus, responsible for memory formation, is believed to play a role in creating memories linked to pleasurable experiences, such as the taste of a favorite food or the sensation of being in love (Davidson & Irwin, 1999). In this way, the hippocampus contributes to the lasting emotional impact of pleasurable events. The limbic system is a complex network of brain structures vital for processing the emotional and motivational aspects of pleasure. The activation of these regions in response to rewarding stimuli is a crucial component of pleasure experiences. A deeper understanding of the limbic system's functioning can enhance our comprehension of pleasure's nature and its influence on human behavior and decision-making.[3.4]

THE BASAL GANGLIA & HEDONIC ASPECTS OF PLEASURE

The basal ganglia, a collection of nuclei situated at the base of the brain, hold a pivotal function in processing reward and motivation. Specifically, the ventral striatum, an integral part of the basal ganglia, has been associated with the processing of hedonic aspects of pleasure, such as the subjective experience of pleasure or reward (Berridge & Kringelbach, 2013). Research has demonstrated that the ventral striatum is activated in response to a variety of pleasurable stimuli, encompassing food, sex, and drugs (Everitt & Robbins, 2016). Moreover, dysfunction in this brain region has been connected to various mental health disorders, including addiction and depression (Nestler & Carlezon, 2006). Additionally, research has indicated that the basal ganglia, incorporating the ventral striatum, participate in reinforcement learning. Reinforcement learning entails the acquisition of new behaviors through trial and error, reinforcing or rewarding behavior that results in positive outcomes (Schultz, 2006). The basal ganglia play a crucial role in this process, with the ventral striatum being especially involved in processing positive feedback or reward (Frank, Seeberger, & O'Reilly, 2004). This positive reinforcement makes the behavior more likely to recur.

The basal ganglia, particularly the ventral striatum, are vital for processing the hedonic aspects of pleasure and reinforcement learning. Dysfunction in this brain region can profoundly impact reward processing and motivation, leading to a range of mental health disorders. Comprehending the underlying mechanisms of the basal ganglia can contribute to the development of novel treatments for these disorders.[3.5]

DYSREGULATION OF THE BRAIN'S PLEASURE CIRCUITRY [3.6]

The brain's pleasure circuitry is a complex system that governs reward-related behavior and responds to various stimuli, including food, sex, social interactions, and drugs of abuse. Comprehending the neural mechanisms underlying pleasure and reward-related behaviors is essential for devising effective treatments for addiction, depression, and other psychiatric disorders. Studies employing neuroimaging techniques have revealed that activating the brain's reward system, particularly the mesolimbic dopamine system, is linked to the subjective experience of pleasure and reward (Kringelbach & Berridge, 2010). Nonetheless, dysregulation of the brain's pleasure circuitry can result in significant negative outcomes, such as addiction, depression, anxiety, and schizophrenia. For instance, addiction is characterized by compulsive drug use despite adverse consequences and is associated with changes in the brain's reward system, including dopamine release and receptor availability (Volkow et al., 2016). Similarly, depression involves decreased activity in the pleasure circuitry, including the ventral striatum and prefrontal cortex, contributing to the anhedonic symptoms of the disorder (Snaith et al., 1995). Anxiety disorders, including generalized anxiety disorder and social anxiety disorder, also exhibit alterations in the brain's reward system, featuring increased amygdala activation and decreased ventral striatum activation (Paulus & Stein, 2006). Schizophrenia, characterized by alterations in dopamine function and brain region connectivity, is another disorder influenced by the dysregulation of the pleasure circuitry, affecting both positive and negative symptoms (Howes & Kapur, 2014). Dysregulation of the brain's pleasure circuitry can also contribute to other maladaptive behaviors, such as compulsive gambling and overeating (Dreher & Schmidt, 2008; Volkow et al., 2013). These behaviors are associated with increased activation in the brain's reward system, which can lead to a loss of control and negative consequences. Hence, understanding the mechanisms of dysregulation in the brain's pleasure circuitry is crucial for developing effective interventions and treatments for a range of psychiatric and behavioral disorders.

<u>Real-Life Examples of Dysregulation:</u>

1. <u>Addiction</u>: Dysregulation of the brain's pleasure circuitry has been linked to addiction, characterized by compulsive drug-seeking behavior despite adverse consequences. Research has shown that drugs of abuse, such as cocaine and heroin, activate the brain's reward system and can lead to long-term changes in the brain's structure and function (Koob & Volkow, 2016).

2. <u>Depression</u>: Dysregulation of the brain's pleasure circuitry has also been implicated in depression, characterized by a persistent feeling of sadness or loss of interest in activities that were once pleasurable. Research has shown that individuals with depression have decreased activity in the brain's reward system, which may contribute to their reduced ability to experience pleasure (Nestler & Carlezon, 2006).

3. <u>Eating disorders</u>: Dysregulation of the brain's pleasure circuitry has also been associated with eating disorders like anorexia and bulimia nervosa. Research has shown that individuals with eating disorders have altered brain activity in the reward system, possibly contributing to their disordered eating behaviors (Frank et al., 2012).

4. <u>Gambling addiction</u>: Dysregulation of the brain's pleasure circuitry has also been implicated in gambling addiction, characterized by a persistent and recurrent pattern of gambling behavior despite adverse consequences. Research has shown that gambling activates the brain's reward system and can change the brain's

structure and function (Potenza, 2008).

5. <u>Hypersexuality</u>: Dysregulation of the brain's pleasure circuitry has also been associated with hypersexuality, characterized by a persistent and intense preoccupation with sexual thoughts, fantasies, or behaviors that interfere with daily functioning. Research has shown that individuals with hypersexuality have altered brain activity in the reward system, possibly contributing to their excessive sexual behavior (Gola et al., 2017).

6. <u>Binge eating disorder</u>: Binge eating disorder is a type of eating disorder characterized by episodes of uncontrollable eating. Research has shown that the brain's reward and pleasure circuits may be dysregulated in individuals with this disorder, leading to compulsive overeating (Voon et al., 2015).

7. <u>Gambling addiction</u>: Gambling addiction is a behavioral addiction characterized by a persistent and recurrent gambling behavior that disrupts personal, family, or vocational pursuits. Neuroimaging studies have shown that individuals with gambling addiction have dysregulation of the brain's reward and pleasure circuits, which may contribute to the development and maintenance of this disorder (Linnet et al., 2011).

8. <u>Sexual addiction</u>: Sexual addiction is a behavioral addiction characterized by compulsive and excessive sexual behavior. Research has shown that individuals with sexual addiction may have dysregulation of the brain's reward and pleasure circuits, which may contribute to the development and maintenance of this disorder (Kühn and Gallinat, 2016).

9. <u>Exercise addiction</u>: Exercise addiction is a behavioral addiction characterized by a compulsive and excessive exercise pattern that interferes with regular daily activities. Neuroimaging studies have shown that individuals with exercise addiction have dysregulation of the brain's reward and pleasure circuits, which may contribute to the development and maintenance of this disorder (Smith et al., 2015).

10. <u>Internet addiction</u>: Internet addiction is a behavioral addiction characterized by excessive or compulsive use of the internet, which interferes with daily life. Research has shown that individuals with internet addiction may have dysregulation of the brain's reward and pleasure circuits, which may contribute to the development and maintenance of this disorder (Kuss and Griffiths, 2012).

Dysregulation of the brain's pleasure circuitry can result in numerous detrimental outcomes, including addiction, depression, anxiety, eating disorders, and other mental health challenges. These conditions can considerably affect an individual's quality of life and yield long-term consequences if not addressed. Preventative strategies targeting dysregulation of the pleasure circuitry necessitate identifying and addressing underlying risk factors, such as genetic predispositions, trauma, and environmental influences. Early intervention and treatment are vital for mitigating the development of these conditions, potentially incorporating psychotherapy, medication management, or a combination thereof. Education and awareness campaigns can further encourage healthy habits and diminish the stigma surrounding mental health issues. Moreover, fostering healthy lifestyle habits, including regular exercise, a balanced diet, and stress management, can contribute to regulating the brain's pleasure circuitry and lowering the risk of developing addictive behaviors or mental health disorders. Social support and positive social interactions serve as protective factors against dysregulation of the pleasure circuitry, as isolation and loneliness heighten mental health problem risks. Addressing dysregulation of the pleasure circuitry early and implementing effective prevention strategies are crucial to minimizing the negative impact of these conditions on individuals and society. By promoting a holistic approach that considers individual and societal factors, we can foster a healthier and more contented community.

<u>10 Major Prevention Strategies Regarding Dysregulation of Pleasure:</u>

1. <u>Education</u>: Educating individuals on the risks associated with the dysregulation of pleasure, such as addiction and mental health disorders, can help raise awareness and promote healthier choices (Sussman & Arnett, 2014).

2. <u>Early intervention</u>: Identifying and addressing dysregulation of pleasure early on can help prevent more severe problems (Becker et al., 2016).

3. <u>Behavioral therapy</u>: Behavioral therapy, such as cognitive-behavioral therapy, can help individuals learn healthy coping strategies and develop alternative ways of experiencing pleasure (Marhe et al., 2013).

4. <u>Mindfulness meditation</u>: Mindfulness meditation can help individuals regulate their emotions and increase their awareness of the present moment, reducing the risk of dysregulation of pleasure (Garland et al., 2015).

5. <u>Support groups</u>: Support groups, such as Alcoholics Anonymous and Narcotics Anonymous, can provide individuals with social support and encouragement to

help them overcome dysregulation of pleasure (Kelly et al., 2012).

6. <u>Family therapy</u>: Family therapy can help address underlying family dynamics that may contribute to the dysregulation of pleasure and promote healthier communication and relationships (O'Farrell et al., 2019).

7. <u>Pharmacotherapy</u>: Medications, such as antidepressants and antipsychotics, can treat underlying mental health disorders that may contribute to the dysregulation of pleasure (Hawton & van Heeringen, 2009).

8. <u>Exercise</u>: Regular exercise can help promote a healthy release of endorphins and other pleasurable neurotransmitters, reducing the risk of dysregulation of pleasure (Lindner et al., 2019).

9. <u>Stress reduction techniques</u>: Stress reduction techniques, such as yoga and deep breathing, can help individuals manage stress and reduce the risk of using dysregulated pleasure-seeking behaviors as a coping mechanism (Katz et al., 2019).

10. <u>Harm reduction</u>: Harm reduction approaches, such as providing clean needles to prevent the spread of disease among injection drug users, can help reduce the negative consequences associated with dysregulated pleasure-seeking behaviors (Volkow & Baler, 2014).

Utilizing various prevention strategies, individuals and communities can collaborate to mitigate the adverse effects of pleasure dysregulation and foster healthier, more fulfilling lives. In summary, prevention strategies encompass a diverse array of approaches, including education and awareness campaigns, early intervention programs, psychotherapy and counseling, medication-assisted treatments, and lifestyle modifications. These strategies address the myriad factors contributing to pleasure dysregulation, such as genetic predisposition, environmental stressors, social and cultural influences, and personal coping mechanisms. Education and awareness campaigns can enhance individuals' understanding of the risks and consequences associated with addictive and compulsive behaviors, offering information on healthy alternatives for pleasure-seeking. Early intervention programs, incorporating screening and assessment tools, can identify individuals at risk for pleasure dysregulation, enabling timely interventions to prevent addiction or other mental health challenges. Psychotherapy and counseling approaches, like cognitive-behavioral therapy and motivational interviewing, can assist individuals in cultivating healthy coping strategies and pinpointing triggers for pleasure-seeking behaviors. Medication-assisted treatments, encompassing opioid agonists and nicotine replacement therapy, can alleviate cravings and withdrawal symptoms related to addiction. Lifestyle modifications, including regular exercise, nutritious eating habits, and stress management techniques, further promote overall well-being and decrease the risk of pleasure dysregulation. It is essential to recognize that prevention necessitates a commitment to continuous education, research, and innovation within the realms of addiction and mental health.

<u>NEUROTRANSMITTERS AND PLEASURE</u> [4]

Neurotransmitters, chemical messengers facilitating communication between neurons in the brain and body, play a vital role in modulating mood, cognition, and behavior. They are intricately involved in the experience of pleasure, with key neurotransmitters including dopamine, serotonin, and endorphins. Dopamine is associated with pleasure and reward, released in response to positive experiences such as eating, socializing, and participating in enjoyable activities. Serotonin governs mood and correlates with feelings of happiness and well-being, while endorphins, natural painkillers released during exercise or physically demanding activities, are connected to pleasure and euphoria. Imbalances in these neurotransmitters may result in various mental health disorders, such as depression, anxiety, and addiction. For instance, reduced dopamine levels have been linked to depression, while elevated dopamine levels are implicated in addiction. Comprehending the roles of neurotransmitters in pleasure and other facets of mental health is crucial for devising effective treatments for mental health disorders. Interventions like psychotherapy, medication, and other therapeutic approaches can reestablish neurotransmitter equilibrium and alleviate mental health disorder symptoms.

Several neurotransmitters, including dopamine, serotonin, and endorphins, are involved in the experience of pleasure. These chemical messengers in the brain play a pivotal role in regulating various physiological and psychological functions. Dopamine, critical for the brain's reward system, is associated with pleasure, motivation, and learning (Berridge & Kringelbach, 2015). Serotonin is implicated in mood regulation, influencing feelings of well-being and pleasure (Blier & El Mansari, 2013). Endorphins, produced in response to stress or pain, evoke feelings of pleasure and euphoria (Zubieta et al., 2001). Dopamine has been demonstrated to be involved in pleasure derived from a wide range of activities, such as food, sex, drugs, and social interactions (Kringelbach & Berridge, 2010). Dopamine signaling deficits have been linked to various psychiatric disorders, including addiction and depression (Nestler & Carlezon, 2006). Likewise, serotonin is connected to pleasure experienced through social bonding and rewards, including recognition and status (Crockett et al., 2008). Deficits in serotonin signaling are associated with psychiatric disorders, such as depression and anxiety (Harmer, 2008). Endorphins are also implicated in pleasure derived from physical activities, like exercise (Craft & Perna, 2004). The interplay between these neurotransmitters is intricate and depends on context and individual factors. For instance, dopamine release in response to pleasurable stimuli can be modulated by other neurotransmitters, including glutamate and GABA (Grace, 2000). Moreover, the effects of serotonin on pleasure can be influenced by genetic and environmental factors, such as stress and trauma (Caspi et al., 2003). Studying neurotransmitters and their roles in the experience of pleasure remains an active area of neuroscience research, holding significant implications for treating psychiatric disorders and promoting mental health and well-being.

Serotonin, a neurotransmitter associated with mood regulation, is involved in the experience of pleasure and has been implicated in various mental health disorders, including depression and anxiety. It is believed to play a role in processing social rewards, such as social bonding and affiliation, and its activation is linked to positive social behaviors (Zaki & Williams, 2013). Serotonin is also implicated in regulating appetite and sleep, and is often targeted by antidepressant medications (Harmer & Cowen, 2013). Blier and Abbott's (2001) study found that the selective serotonin reuptake inhibitor (SSRI) fluoxetine increased extracellular serotonin levels in rats' prefrontal cortex, suggesting enhanced serotonergic activity in the brain. Endorphins, a class of neuropeptides, are involved in regulating pain and the experience of pleasure. Released during rewarding or pleasurable activities like exercise or sexual activity, endorphins produce feelings of euphoria and pain relief. They interact with opioid receptors in the brain, resulting in both analgesic and rewarding effects (Bryant & Dunlop, 2019). Binding to the same receptors as opioids like morphine, endorphins can induce analgesia and euphoria (Pfeiffer et al., 1986). Koepp et al. (1998) used positron emission tomography (PET) to demonstrate that endogenous endorphins were released in the brain during pleasurable experiences, such as listening to music or viewing paintings, suggesting their involvement in the brain's reward system. Dopamine is a neurotransmitter that plays a crucial role in the brain's reward and motivation systems. It is released in response to pleasurable stimuli, reinforcing the behavior that led to its release. For example, a study by Schultz et al. (1997) found that dopamine neurons in the brain of monkeys responded to a reward signal, such as juice or food, which suggests that dopamine is involved in encoding reward prediction and processing reward reward-related information. Understanding the role of neurotransmitters in the experience of pleasure can help researchers develop treatments for psychological disorders and addiction by targeting specific neurotransmitter systems. For example, medications that target the dopaminergic system, such as dopamine agonists or antagonists, have been used to treat addiction and Parkinson's disease (Volkow et al., 2016). Similarly, medications that target the serotonergic system, such as SSRIs, are commonly used to treat depression and anxiety (Harmer & Cowen, 2013). Studying neurotransmitters and their role in the brain's pleasure circuitry has important implications for understanding human behavior and developing effective interventions.

Additionally, the endorphin system, a distinct neurotransmitter system, plays a crucial role in modulating pain perception and the experience of pleasure. Endorphins, which are endogenous opioid peptides, can be released during a variety of pleasurable experiences, including exercise and sexual activity. These peptides serve as natural painkillers, eliciting feelings of euphoria and well-being (Bryant & Dunlop, 2019). The release of endorphins is facilitated by the activation of mu-opioid receptors in the brain, which can induce both analgesic and rewarding effects (Pfeiffer et al., 1986).

Notably, research has shown that endorphins also play a role in mediating social bonding and attachment. For instance, studies have found that endorphin release is associated with positive social interactions, such as laughter, touch, and grooming, which are crucial for fostering social cohesion and maintaining group dynamics (Dunbar & Shultz, 2010). This highlights the importance of pleasure as a driving force in social relationships, as it may enhance affiliative behaviors and contribute to the development and maintenance of social bonds. Moreover, endorphins have been implicated in the neurobiological basis of social attachment, as they share similarities with exogenous opioids, which are known to play a role in attachment formation (Machin & Dunbar, 2011). Endorphins may help reinforce social bonds by increasing feelings of pleasure and reward associated with social interactions, thereby strengthening the emotional connection between individuals (Nummenmaa et al., 2016). Understanding the role of endorphins in the experience of pleasure and social relationships may provide valuable insights into the neurobiological underpinnings of human social behavior and inform the development of novel therapeutic interventions for mental health disorders characterized by social dysfunction, such as depression and social anxiety disorder.

Pleasure is an intricate and multidimensional phenomenon that encompasses a myriad of brain regions and neurotransmitter systems. Gaining a comprehensive understanding of the mechanisms that underlie pleasure can have significant implications for diverse fields such as psychology, neuroscience, and philosophy. By delving deeper into the complexities of pleasure and its regulation, the potential to develop more effective treatments for psychiatric disorders, addiction, and other compulsive behaviors becomes increasingly plausible. Furthermore, learning to regulate and balance our personal experiences of pleasure can contribute to a happier and healthier lifestyle. Investigating the release of endorphins in relation to pleasurable experiences, such as exercise, laughter, and social bonding, provides valuable insights into the complex dynamics of pleasure. For instance, research has demonstrated that individuals who engage in regular physical activity experience an increase in endorphins, which may underlie the mood-enhancing effects of exercise (Craft & Perna, 2004). Additionally, the role of endorphins in social bonding and well-being highlights the importance of interpersonal connections in our pursuit of pleasure. By understanding the neurobiological basis of pleasurable experiences, we can foster more enriching relationships and cultivate greater life satisfaction. This knowledge can also inform interventions designed to improve social functioning in individuals with psychiatric disorders, ultimately enhancing their overall quality of life. The study of pleasure is crucial in advancing our understanding of human behavior, emotion, and mental health. By continuing to explore the intricate processes underlying pleasure, we can work towards developing more effective treatments for various psychological disorders, promote healthier lifestyles, and foster greater well-being in individuals and communities alike.

In a similar vein, laughter has been shown to stimulate endorphin release, resulting in a heightened sense of euphoria and well-being (Dunbar et al., 2012). Moreover, social bonding activities, such as embracing or engaging in quality time with loved ones, have been linked to increased endorphin release, potentially contributing to a sense of closeness and happiness (Nummenmaa et al., 2016). Comprehending the role of neurotransmitters in pleasure can provide valuable insights for the development of treatments targeting mental health disorders characterized by dysregulation of the pleasure system. For instance, medications addressing dopamine, like those utilized in the treatment of Parkinson's disease, have demonstrated efficacy in the management of depression (Blier & El Mansari, 2013). In a similar manner, medications targeting serotonin, such as selective serotonin reuptake inhibitors (SSRIs), have proven effective in alleviating symptoms of depression and anxiety (Cipriani et al., 2018). Additionally, non-pharmacological interventions that promote endorphin release, including exercise, laughter, and social bonding, have been shown to effectively reduce symptoms of depression and anxiety (Mead et al., 2011; Wipfli et al., 2008). By considering the complex interplay between neurotransmitters and pleasure experiences, researchers and clinicians can develop more targeted and efficacious treatment approaches for various mental health conditions. Furthermore, the promotion of non-pharmacological interventions that harness the power of endorphins can offer a holistic and complementary approach to traditional pharmacological treatments, fostering overall well-being and improved mental health outcomes.

As previously mentioned, endorphins hold a pivotal role as neurotransmitters implicated in the experience of pleasure. These endogenous opioid peptides, synthesized within the body, possess the ability to bind to the same receptors as exogenous opioid drugs, eliciting sensations of pleasure and analgesia. Endorphins are released during a variety of activities, including physical exercise, laughter, and sexual encounters, and are speculated to contribute to the phenomenon known as "runner's high" often reported by athletes. Interestingly, endorphins can also be released during emotionally painful experiences, such as grieving or experiencing social rejection. This release may serve as a coping mechanism, providing emotional relief and solace in times of distress (Hsu et al., 2013). This endorphin-mediated response may have evolved as an adaptive function, fostering social bonding and resilience in the face of adversity (Panksepp et al., 1980). The multifaceted nature of endorphin release and its impact on our emotional and physical experiences underscores the importance of continued research into the complex interplay between these neurotransmitters and human behavior. By expanding our understanding of endorphins and their role in the modulation of pleasure and pain, researchers can potentially uncover novel therapeutic interventions to address mental health disorders, chronic pain, and addiction, ultimately promoting enhanced well-being and quality of life.

Another notable neurotransmitter implicated in the experience of pleasure is oxytocin, frequently dubbed the "love hormone" due to its significant role in social bonding and attachment processes. Oxytocin is released during a range of intimate human interactions, encompassing sexual encounters, breastfeeding, and physical touch, such as hugging (Magon & Kalra, 2011). Oxytocin has been demonstrated to facilitate trust, social bonding, and attachment, contributing to the pleasure derived from these interpersonal experiences (Bartz et al., 2011). Its effects extend beyond the realm of social interactions, with research suggesting that oxytocin is involved in regulating stress response, reducing anxiety, and promoting a sense of calm and well-being (Neumann & Slattery, 2016) Emerging evidence indicates that oxytocin may harbor therapeutic potential for the treatment of mood disorders, including anxiety and depression. For instance, studies have shown that oxytocin administration can alleviate symptoms of anxiety and depression in animal models, as well as improve social functioning in individuals with autism spectrum disorder (Yatawara et al., 2016; Lukas et al., 2011). Given the multifaceted influence of oxytocin on pleasure, social behavior, and emotional regulation, continued research into its underlying mechanisms and potential clinical applications is warranted. A deeper understanding of oxytocin's role in human behavior and mental health could pave the way for innovative therapeutic interventions, enhancing well-being and fostering healthier interpersonal connections.

A multitude of neurotransmitters contribute to the intricate experience of pleasure, encompassing dopamine, serotonin, endorphins, and oxytocin. These neurotransmitters serve vital functions across a wide array of pleasure-related processes, such as the anticipation, appraisal, and hedonic enjoyment of rewards, in addition to social bonding and attachment (Berridge & Kringelbach, 2015; Bartz et al., 2011). Each neurotransmitter exhibits distinct yet interconnected roles in the realm of pleasure. Dopamine, for instance, is associated with the brain's reward system, motivation, and learning (Berridge & Kringelbach, 2015). Serotonin, on the other hand, is involved in mood regulation and the perception of social rewards, including social bonding and affiliation (Zaki & Williams, 2013). Endorphins, a group of endogenous opioid peptides, contribute to feelings of euphoria, pain relief, and well-being in response to rewarding or pleasurable activities (Craft & Perna, 2004). Lastly, oxytocin plays a significant part in social bonding, attachment, and trust, thereby affecting the pleasure derived from interpersonal experiences (Bartz et al., 2011). Delving into the roles of these neurotransmitters in pleasure can provide researchers and clinicians with invaluable insights for the development of more effective treatments targeting addiction, mood disorders, and other conditions linked to pleasure dysregulation. By enhancing our understanding of the complex interactions and functions of these neurotransmitter systems, we can pave the way for innovative therapeutic interventions that address the underlying neurobiological mechanisms of pleasure-related disorders, ultimately improving mental health and overall well-being.

<u>THE PSYCHOLOGY OF PLEASURE</u>

The psychology of pleasure is an intricate and multidimensional subject, garnering interest from researchers across a wide array of disciplines. Pleasure is commonly defined as a subjective feeling of enjoyment or satisfaction that emerges from experiencing specific stimuli or engaging in particular activities (Kringelbach & Berridge, 2010). Pleasure manifests in diverse forms, including physical, emotional, intellectual, and social domains. The investigation of pleasure delves into the cognitive, neural, and behavioral processes that underpin its experience. A primary theory in this area is the hedonic theory, proposing that pleasure serves as the fundamental motivator of human behavior (Kringelbach & Berridge, 2010). According to this perspective, individuals are driven to pursue pleasure and evade pain, rendering the quest for pleasure the ultimate objective of all human actions. Empirical evidence supporting this theory can be observed through research on the brain's reward system, implicated in the experience of pleasure and activated by a range of stimuli, such as food, sex, drugs, and social interactions (Berridge & Kringelbach, 2015). An essential facet of the psychology of pleasure concerns the role of individual differences in the experience of pleasure. Studies have demonstrated that people exhibit varying sensitivities to pleasurable stimuli and abilities to derive pleasure from distinct activities (Kringelbach & Berridge, 2010). For instance, some individuals may find greater pleasure in social interactions, while others may prefer intellectual pursuits. Furthermore, the experience of pleasure is subject to numerous contextual factors, including cultural norms, social expectations, and situational variables (Kringelbach & Berridge, 2010). Consequently, certain activities or behaviors may be deemed pleasurable in one culture but not in another, and individuals may encounter differing levels of pleasure contingent upon the social context. The psychology of pleasure bears significant implications for comprehending human behavior and well-being. Research indicates that the experience of pleasure is associated with a variety of positive outcomes, encompassing enhanced mood, increased motivation, and improved cognitive functioning (Berridge & Kringelbach, 2015). However, the pursuit of pleasure may also yield negative consequences, such as addiction, risky behavior, and impaired judgment (Kringelbach & Berridge, 2010). The psychology of pleasure represents a complex and multifaceted topic, extensively studied by researchers from diverse disciplines. The experience of pleasure is influenced by an array of cognitive, neural, and behavioral processes, individual differences, and contextual factors. Understanding the psychology of pleasure is crucial for promoting human well-being and mitigating adverse outcomes linked to the pursuit of pleasure.[5]

Reflective Questions:

1. How does understanding the neurobiological mechanisms underlying pleasure impact your perspective on the experiences and activities that bring you pleasure? In what ways might this knowledge influence your pursuit of pleasure moving forward?

2. In light of the science of pleasure, how can we differentiate between healthy and potentially harmful sources of pleasure? How can this awareness guide us in making more informed decisions about the activities and experiences we choose to engage in?

3. How can the insights from the science of pleasure be applied to improve our well-being and overall quality of life? Are there specific strategies or practices that you could implement in your own life to enhance your experience of pleasure and happiness?

4. Considering the role of neurotransmitters, such as dopamine and serotonin, in the experience of pleasure, how might this knowledge inform our understanding of addictive behaviors or the pursuit of instant gratification? How can we strike a balance between seeking pleasure and maintaining long-term well-being?

5. In what ways can the science of pleasure contribute to the development of more effective interventions and therapies for individuals struggling with mental health issues, such as depression or anxiety? How might a deeper understanding of the neurobiology of pleasure inform new approaches to promoting mental health and emotional resilience?

PHILOSOPHY OF PLEASURE

Philosophers have exhibited a longstanding interest in the nature and significance of pleasure. The philosophy of pleasure can be traced back to ancient Greek philosophers, such as Epicurus and Aristotle, who posited that pleasure constitutes the ultimate aim of human life. In contemporary times, philosophers persist in investigating the nature and value of pleasure, probing its essence, goodness, and pursuit. This overview will examine the philosophy of pleasure, incorporating foundational texts and ideas within the field. A central inquiry in the philosophy of pleasure concerns its essence. Scholars have proposed various conceptualizations of pleasure, encompassing physical sensations, mental states, and evaluative judgments. One prominent perspective is the hedonistic theory of pleasure, which contends that pleasure is an intrinsic, non-instrumental good sought for its own sake. According to this view, pleasure is a feeling of satisfaction or enjoyment that emerges when we fulfill our desires or attain something we value. Philosophers such as Jeremy Bentham and John Stuart Mill have defended the hedonistic theory of pleasure, asserting that pleasure should constitute the ultimate goal of moral action. An alternative perspective on pleasure is represented by the evaluative theory, which posits that pleasure signifies a positive appraisal of an object or experience. From this standpoint, pleasure is not merely a feeling or sensation but also entails making judgments regarding the value or quality of something. Proponents of this perspective, such as G. E. Moore, argue that pleasure is an essential and indivisible attribute of experiences. A critical question within the philosophy of pleasure pertains to whether pleasure is intrinsically good. While some philosophers endorse the inherent value of pleasure, others dispute this notion, suggesting that pleasure's worth is merely instrumental or can even be harmful under specific circumstances. A critique of the hedonistic approach to pleasure, for example, highlights its failure to address the ethical significance of activities that may not necessarily produce pleasure, such as altruistic acts or the pursuit of knowledge. Several philosophers maintain that pleasure's value is strictly instrumental, functioning as a means to achieve a distinct end. Aristotle, for instance, proposed that pleasure arises as a byproduct of virtuous activities, possessing value only insofar as it contributes to a morally virtuous life. Similarly, some contemporary philosophers argue that pleasure is valuable solely for its capacity to promote overall well-being or happiness.

Conversely, several philosophers challenge the assumption that pleasure is inherently positive, arguing that it can be detrimental when it results in addiction, hedonism, or distracts from more profound values. Critics of the hedonistic conception of pleasure emphasize its ephemeral and unreliable nature, which can occasionally conflict with other values such as justice or responsibility. A third pivotal inquiry in the philosophy of pleasure concerns the appropriate pursuit of pleasure. While some philosophers advocate for seeking pleasure at all costs, others propose pursuing pleasure in moderation or balancing it against other values. For instance, the ancient Greek philosopher Epicurus posited that pleasure should be sought rationally and judiciously, evading excess or overindulgence. Similarly, Aristotle maintained that pleasure ought to be pursued in moderation within the context of a virtuous life. Contemporary philosophers have also examined the question of pursuing pleasure. Some argue for seeking pleasure in ways that align with our values or foster overall well-being. Others propose exploring a variety of pleasures, rather than concentrating solely on physical or sensory experiences. Moreover, some philosophers advocate pursuing pleasure in ways that contribute to personal growth or self-realization. The philosophy of pleasure constitutes a rich and intricate field that raises fundamental questions about the nature and significance of human experience. While philosophers have offered diverse accounts of pleasure, many concur that pleasure is an essential component of a fulfilling life. Nonetheless, an ongoing debate persists regarding whether pleasure is intrinsically valuable and the manner in which it should be pursued. Some scholars contend that the pursuit of pleasure should be balanced against other values, such as virtue or responsibility, while others argue for a measured and rational approach. Furthermore, some philosophers consider pleasure as part of a broader pursuit of human flourishing and self-realization. The philosophy of pleasure continues to provide critical insights into the nature and value of human experience, with potential implications for fields ranging from ethics and aesthetics to psychology and neuroscience.

THE HISTORY OF PLEASURE IN PHILOSOPHY

The history of pleasure in philosophy has deep roots dating back to ancient times and has captivated numerous philosophers. These thinkers have examined various aspects of pleasure, such as its essence, its role in human life, and its connection to happiness. This book will present an overview of the history of pleasure in philosophy, emphasizing some of the most notable philosophical perspectives on this subject. Ancient Greek philosophy offers some of the earliest philosophical discussions on pleasure. The Epicureans, a school of philosophy established by Epicurus, posited that pleasure was the ultimate objective of human life, and happiness could be attained through its pursuit (Konstan, 2018). Epicurus differentiated between two types of pleasure: static and kinetic. Static pleasure refers to the absence of pain or disturbance, while kinetic pleasure is the active experience of pleasure. Epicurus argued that the pursuit of static pleasure was the key to achieving happiness. In contrast, the Stoics maintained that pleasure was not the ultimate aim of human life. They emphasized the significance of virtue and asserted that pleasure should be subordinate to virtue (Inwood, 2005). The Stoics considered pleasure to be an ephemeral and unreliable emotion, easily disrupted by external events. They posited that true happiness could only be achieved by cultivating virtuous character and living in accordance with reason.During the medieval period, pleasure was frequently associated with sin and seen as a threat to spiritual salvation. Christian philosopher Augustine of Hippo contended that pleasure was a distraction from the pursuit of God and that genuine happiness could only be found in God (Gavin, 2008). Augustine argued that human desires were inherently sinful, and indulging in pleasure could result in moral degradation. In the modern era, philosophers have continued to investigate questions surrounding pleasure. Jeremy Bentham, a prominent figure in this area, developed the philosophy of utilitarianism. Bentham asserted that the pursuit of pleasure should be the ultimate goal of human life and that actions should be assessed based on their capacity to promote pleasure and minimize pain (Bentham, 1789). Bentham's philosophy profoundly influenced social and political thought, particularly in formulating policies that promote the greatest happiness for the largest number of people. The philosophical exploration of pleasure boasts a rich and diverse history, spanning from ancient Greece to the modern era. Philosophers have delved into a variety of questions regarding pleasure, encompassing its nature, its role in human life, and its relationship to happiness. The philosophical perspectives on pleasure are wide-ranging, from advocating for pleasure as the ultimate goal of life to advocating for pleasure's subordination to virtue. The history of pleasure in philosophy offers a rich mosaic of thought on this critical facet of human experience.

THE HEDONISTIC APPROACH TO PLEASURE

The Hedonistic approach to pleasure is a philosophical doctrine asserting that pleasure is the ultimate objective of human life. This perspective finds its origins in the teachings of ancient Greek philosophers such as Epicurus and Aristippus, who posited that happiness and fulfillment are derived from experiencing pleasure and evading pain. This approach to pleasure has been subject to extensive debate and discourse throughout history and remains a prominent topic in contemporary philosophy. Epicureanism, established by Epicurus, constituted a central philosophical school in ancient Greece that promoted pleasure as the ultimate aim of human life. Epicurus maintained that pleasure is the highest good, and all human actions should serve to maximize pleasure and minimize pain. However, he did not advocate for indulging in reckless or excessive pleasure-seeking. Epicurus valued moderation and prioritized the pursuit of long-term pleasure over fleeting, transient pleasures.

Conversely, Aristippus, a disciple of Socrates, founded the philosophy of Hedonism. This belief system posits that pleasure is the sole intrinsic good, and every human action should be geared toward maximizing pleasure and minimizing pain. Aristippus contended that individuals should pursue pleasure without limits or restrictions, provided it does not inflict harm on oneself or others. The hedonistic approach to pleasure has encountered substantial debate in philosophical circles. Detractors argue that it constitutes a superficial and self-centered philosophy, overemphasizing personal pleasure while neglecting the significance of other moral values, such as justice, compassion, and duty. Furthermore, critics assert that the pursuit of pleasure can result in addiction and dependency, ultimately culminating in dissatisfaction and unhappiness. Nevertheless, the hedonistic approach to pleasure persists as a prevalent topic in contemporary philosophy. Numerous philosophers contend that pleasure is an essential element of a meaningful life and that individuals should endeavor to experience it in a healthy and responsible manner. For instance, philosopher John Stuart Mill maintained that the principle of the greatest happiness should inform the pursuit of pleasure to benefit the largest number of people. The goal should be to cultivate a society that optimizes pleasure for all individuals. The hedonistic approach to pleasure is a philosophical doctrine that posits pleasure as the ultimate goal of human life. Although this approach has faced criticism for its emphasis on personal pleasure and potential for addiction and dependency, many philosophers maintain that pleasure is a vital component of a meaningful life and that individuals should strive to experience it in a healthy and responsible manner.

THE IMPORTANCE OF BALANCE IN PLEASURE

Pleasure is a fundamental component of human existence, stemming from various sources such as food, sex, socializing, and entertainment (Kringelbach & Berridge, 2012). Nevertheless, excessive engagement in pleasurable activities can result in addiction, obsession, and other detrimental consequences. While pleasure-seeking activities are crucial for a fulfilling life, it is essential to balance them with other vital aspects of life to prevent adverse effects (Stucki & Rihs-Middel, 2017). Physical health can be negatively impacted by excessive indulgence in pleasurable activities. Overeating, for example, can lead to obesity, diabetes, and cardiovascular diseases (Lindemann, 2020), while substance abuse can harm vital organs and increase the risk of cancer and infections (Koob, 2019). Sedentary pleasures, such as watching television or playing video games, can contribute to obesity, hypertension, and musculoskeletal disorders (Biddle et al., 2019). Therefore, balance is crucial to ensure pleasure does not compromise physical health. Mental health can benefit from pleasure, as it can reduce stress, improve mood, and enhance cognitive function (Laukka et al., 2021). However, excessive pleasure-seeking can lead to addiction, a mental disorder characterized by compulsive and harmful behaviors (American Psychiatric Association, 2013). Addiction can cause psychological distress, impair social and occupational functioning, and distract individuals from essential life goals and responsibilities, leading to guilt, shame, and regret (Koob, 2019; Elster, 2019). Thus, maintaining a balance is vital for preserving mental health and avoiding the negative consequences of pleasure-seeking. Social well-being can also be enhanced by pleasure, as it promotes interaction, bonding, and intimacy (Laukka et al., 2021). However, prioritizing pleasure over relationships may lead to estrangement and loneliness (Koob, 2019). Moreover, some pleasurable activities, such as substance abuse and gambling, can result in negative social consequences, including financial problems, legal issues, and stigma (Lindemann, 2020). Consequently, striking a balance between pleasure-seeking and other aspects of life is essential for overall well-being. Research underscores the importance of balance in pleasure. For instance, Caprara et al. (2012) found that individuals engaging in a balanced combination of pleasure-seeking and other activities experienced higher well-being levels than those solely focused on pleasure-seeking. Similarly, Duckworth et al. (2012) found that individuals who could balance work and leisure activities were more satisfied with their lives. Pleasure-seeking activities are an essential aspect of human life. However, to prevent negative consequences, it is crucial to maintain a balance between these activities and other vital aspects of life, such as work, social relationships, and personal growth. Empirical research demonstrates that individuals who achieve this balance enjoy higher levels of well-being and are more resilient in the face of adversity.

<u>Reflective Questions</u>:

1. How do various philosophical traditions and perspectives on pleasure align with your own personal beliefs and values? Are there specific philosophical ideas or teachings about pleasure that resonate with you or challenge your current understanding?

2. In light of different philosophical approaches to pleasure, how might one strike a balance between seeking pleasure and fulfilling other important aspects of life, such as moral responsibilities, societal obligations, or personal growth?

3. How do historical and cultural contexts influence the development of philosophical perspectives on pleasure? Can you identify any contemporary factors or trends that may shape our current understanding of pleasure and its role in our lives?

4. Reflect on the relationship between pleasure and the concept of the "good life" in various philosophical traditions. How do these ideas inform your personal definition of a fulfilling and meaningful life? Are there specific philosophical principles or practices that you might consider integrating into your own pursuit of happiness?

5. How can engaging with the philosophy of pleasure enhance our understanding of the human experience and inform our approach to seeking pleasure in a mindful and balanced manner? In what ways might the exploration of philosophical perspectives on pleasure contribute to personal growth and self-awareness?

(See "6" in the reference section for all references.)

CULTURAL PERSPECTIVE OF PLEASURE

The concept of pleasure from a cultural perspective posits that an individual's experiences and interpretations of pleasure are significantly influenced by their cultural background and social context. Factors such as values, norms, beliefs, and traditions play a crucial role in shaping how individuals perceive, pursue, and manifest pleasure. A thorough understanding of the cultural aspects of pleasure is vital for disciplines such as psychology, anthropology, sociology, and public health, as this knowledge can contribute to the development of interventions aimed at enhancing well-being and mitigating risk behaviors.

THE CULTURAL APPROACH

The cultural perspective on pleasure emphasizes the significance of an individual's cultural heritage and social environment in shaping their comprehension and appreciation of pleasure. This viewpoint acknowledges that pleasure is a multifaceted phenomenon that cannot be fully understood without considering cultural disparities and variances in social norms and values. This perspective has been investigated across multiple disciplines, such as psychology, anthropology, and sociology. The following five examples demonstrate the importance of the cultural perspective in understanding pleasure:

1. <u>The cultural shaping of sexual pleasure</u>: Sexual pleasure is a profoundly cultural and social phenomenon, and cultural norms and values shape people's experiences and perceptions of sexual pleasure. For example, in some cultures, such as the US, sexual pleasure is often linked to individualism and pursuing pleasure for its own sake. In contrast, in other cultures, such as Japan, sexual pleasure is often associated with maintaining social harmony and preserving group cohesion (Gagnon & Simon, 2005; Lohmus et al., 2015).

2. <u>The influence of cultural traditions on eating</u>: People's pleasure in eating is deeply influenced by cultural traditions, including the types of food consumed, how food is prepared and served, and the social contexts in which food is shared. For example, in some cultures, such as Italy, food is often consumed in a social context, with long meals shared with friends and family, whereas in other cultures, such as the US, food is often consumed on the go or alone (Fischler, 1988; Probyn, 2000).

3. <u>Cultural differences in the experience of music-induced pleasure</u>: Music-induced pleasure is also profoundly influenced by cultural differences in music

preferences and listening practices. For example, music is often associated with religious or spiritual rituals in some cultures, such as India. It can induce a state of trance or ecstasy, whereas, in other cultures, such as the US, music is often associated with entertainment and the pursuit of pleasure (Levitin, 2006; Lonsdale & North, 2011).

4. <u>Cultural variations in sports and physical activity</u>: The pleasure of sports and physical activity is also influenced by cultural norms and values, including the types of sports and physical activities valued by how they are practiced and experienced and their meanings. For example, in some cultures, such as the US, sports are often associated with competition and the pursuit of victory, whereas in other cultures, such as Japan, sports are often seen as a means of self-cultivation and personal improvement (Crossman, 2008; Watanabe & Yamauchi, 2012).

5. <u>The cultural shaping of aesthetic pleasure</u>: Aesthetic pleasure, derived from visual art, literature, and other forms of cultural expression, is also influenced by cultural norms and values. For example, the Western tradition of aesthetics emphasizes the importance of individuality, originality, and creativity, whereas other cultural traditions, such as the Japanese tradition of wabi-sabi, highlight the beauty of imperfection, simplicity, and naturalness (Fukushima, 2005; Zahavi, 2011).

One way that culture influences pleasure is through the socialization of sexual attitudes and behaviors. In many cultures, sex is considered a taboo subject, and expressions of sexual pleasure may be stigmatized or punished. For example, research has shown that in some cultures, female genital mutilation is practiced to control women's sexuality and limit their ability to experience pleasure (Abusharaf, 2006). In other cultures, sexual pleasure is celebrated and even institutionalized, as in the case of ancient Greek and Roman societies, where sexuality was seen as an integral part of life and pleasure was valued as a way to achieve spiritual and physical fulfillment (Foucault, 1984).

Culture plays a significant role in shaping individuals' attitudes and behaviors towards sexuality, which can influence their experiences and pleasure in sexual activities. Here are five examples of how cultural socialization impacts sexual pleasure:

1. <u>Cultural norms around sexual activity</u>: Cultural attitudes towards sexual activity can vary widely, and some cultures may encourage or discourage certain sexual

behaviors. For example, some cultures may view masturbation as taboo or immoral, while others may see it as a healthy and natural sexual expression (Herbenick et al., 2017).

2. <u>Gender and sexual expectations</u>: Cultural expectations around gender roles and sexual behavior can also impact sexual pleasure. For example, in some cultures, men may be expected to be more sexually assertive, while women may be expected to be more passive or submissive (Wood et al., 2020).

3. <u>Cultural beliefs about sexual pleasure</u>: Cultural beliefs about sexual pleasure can also influence how individuals experience sexual activities. For example, some cultures may view sexual pleasure as a necessary component of a healthy sexual relationship, while others may emphasize the importance of sexual self-control and restraint (Chua & Chang, 2016).

4. <u>Cultural taboos and stigmas around sexuality</u>: Cultural taboos and stigmas surrounding sexuality can limit individuals' access to sexual pleasure and impact their attitudes towards sexual expression. For example, in some cultures, same-sex sexual activity may be stigmatized or even criminalized, limiting an individual's ability to experience sexual pleasure (Herek & McLemore, 2013).

5. <u>Cultural differences in sexual education and knowledge</u>: Differences in sexual education and knowledge across cultures can also impact sexual pleasure. For example, some cultures may provide more comprehensive sexual education that includes information on sexual pleasure and consent, while others may provide limited or no sexual education at all (Henderson & Kim, 2016).

The cultural perspective on pleasure extends to various aspects of life, including food, music, and art. Cultural norms and values, for instance, can shape which foods are considered pleasurable, as well as their preparation and consumption methods (Mintz, 1985). In certain cultures, specific foods are linked to rituals and celebrations, and their consumption serves to reinforce social connections and manifest cultural identity (Kittler & Sucher, 2007). Likewise, music and art can elicit pleasure and aesthetic appreciation; however, the standards for beauty or enjoyment can differ across cultures (Dissanayake, 2000).

<u>CULTURE & DOMAINS OF LIFE</u>

The cultural perspective of pleasure is not limited to sexuality but extends to other life domains, including food, music, and art. Here are five examples of how culture shapes pleasure in these areas:

1. <u>Cultural influences on food preferences</u>: Cultural background can shape individuals' preferences for certain types of food and influence their enjoyment of specific tastes, flavors, and textures. For example, some cultures may value spicy or bitter flavors, while others may prefer sweet or savory foods (Provencher et al., 2012).

2. <u>Music preferences and cultural identity</u>: Cultural norms and values can also shape individuals' preferences for different types of music and influence their emotional responses to music. For example, some cultures may place a high value on music as a form of cultural expression and identity, while others may view music primarily as entertainment (Lonsdale & North, 2011).

3. <u>Cultural differences in art appreciation</u>: Cultural background can also shape individuals' appreciation of different art forms and influence their aesthetic preferences. For example, some cultures may value realism and precision in art, while others may prefer abstract or stylized forms of expression (Zahavi, 2011).]

4. <u>Social norms and pleasure in physical activity</u>: Cultural norms and expectations can shape individuals' pleasure and influence their motivation to exercise or sports. For example, some cultures may emphasize the importance of teamwork and group participation in sports, while others may value individual achievement and competition (Crossman, 2008).

5. <u>Cultural differences in pleasure-seeking behaviors</u>: Cultural background can also shape individuals' attitudes towards pleasure-seeking behaviors and influence their decision-making processes. For example, some cultures may place a high value on self-control and restraint, while others may view pleasure-seeking as a legitimate and necessary aspect of life (Ito & Cacioppo, 2018).

Emphasizing the significance of acknowledging the varied human experiences and the influence of culture, the cultural perspective on pleasure provides valuable insights for researchers and practitioners. By comprehending the cultural context in which pleasure is experienced and valued, they can develop culturally sensitive and efficacious interventions to enhance well-being.

DIFFERENT CULTURES AND THEIR APPROACH TO PLEASURE

Distinct cultures possess diverse approaches to pleasure, molded by religious beliefs, social norms, and historical backgrounds. Comprehending these differences fosters cross-cultural understanding and facilitates the development of interventions targeting pleasure-associated health behaviors. Cultural differences in approaches to pleasure are exemplified by attitudes towards alcohol consumption. In some cultures, such as those in the Mediterranean regions, moderate alcohol consumption is integrated into a healthy lifestyle and social interactions (Solecki, 2008). Conversely, in specific Muslim cultures, alcohol is stringently forbidden due to religious convictions (Bukhari, Muslim, Abu-Dawud, & Al-Tirmidhi, 1994). These variations in perspectives on alcohol consumption hold implications for interventions aimed at mitigating alcohol-related harm, necessitating adaptation to particular cultural contexts. An individual's cultural background can shape their attitudes toward alcohol consumption, influencing their experiences and enjoyment associated with drinking. The following are five instances exemplifying cultural variations in approaches to pleasure concerning alcohol:

1. Cultural norms and values pertaining to drinking: Attitudes towards alcohol consumption can differ significantly across cultures. Some societies may regard drinking as an essential aspect of social interaction or celebration, whereas others may perceive it as a source of moral decline (Scheinbaum et al., 2016).

2. Drinking patterns and enjoyment: Cultural norms and values can shape individuals' drinking behaviors, impacting their pleasure derived from alcohol consumption. In certain cultures, drinking primarily occurs in social contexts and may serve to foster community and connections. Conversely, other cultures may approach drinking more individualistically, concentrating on personal gratification (Lau-Barraco & Linden-Carmichael, 2017).

3. Cultural variances in perceptions of intoxication: Cultural norms and expectations can influence individuals' perceptions of alcohol's effects on behavior and pleasure. For instance, some societies might view intoxication as a positive, enjoyable experience, while others may regard it as indicative of weakness or moral failure (Scheffels & Ottersen, 2015).

4. <u>Cultural attitudes towards drinking and gender</u>: Cultural norms and values related to gender roles can shape individuals' attitudes towards alcohol consumption and affect their experiences of pleasure associated with drinking. In some cultures, men may be expected to drink more heavily, showcasing their masculinity through alcohol consumption, while women may be expected to drink less or abstain entirely (Connor et al., 2016).

5. <u>Cultural distinctions in regulating alcohol consumption</u>: Differences in laws, policies, and regulations concerning alcohol consumption can also influence individuals' experiences and enjoyment of drinking. Some cultures may adopt more permissive laws regarding alcohol, while others may enforce more restrictive legislation that limits alcohol's availability and accessibility (Livingston, 2016).

Cultural differences in attitudes towards sexuality are evident across various societies, influencing individuals' experiences and pleasure in sexual activities. These distinctions can also affect the design and implementation of sexual health interventions, necessitating culturally appropriate and sensitive approaches that consider diverse norms and values. Here are five examples illustrating the impact of cultural differences in attitudes toward sexuality on sexual health interventions:

1. <u>Sexual health education</u>: The development and delivery of sexual health education programs must be culturally sensitive and mindful of differing norms and values. For example, a comprehensive sex education program tailored for a Western context might diverge significantly from one designed for a more conservative culture, emphasizing abstinence and modesty (UNESCO, 2018).

2. <u>Communication about sexuality</u>: Varied cultural attitudes towards sexuality can affect the openness with which individuals discuss sexual matters, subsequently influencing their understanding and expression of pleasure. In certain cultures, candid conversations about sexuality might be deemed appropriate, while in others, they could be discouraged or stigmatized (Levine & Coupey, 2003).

3. <u>Gender roles and sexuality</u>: The cultural norms and values surrounding gender roles can shape individuals' attitudes towards sexuality and subsequently affect their experiences of pleasure in sexual activities. Some cultures may adhere to traditional gender roles, prescribing specific expectations for sexual behavior and pleasure, whereas others might promote more egalitarian perspectives

(Connell, 2012).

4. <u>Access to sexual health services</u>: Disparate cultural attitudes towards sexuality can impact access to and utilization of sexual health services. In some contexts, seeking help for sexual health concerns may be considered shameful or stigmatized, potentially deterring individuals from accessing necessary information and services (Pulerwitz et al., 2015).

5. <u>Tailoring interventions to cultural contexts</u>: Understanding the cultural context and recognizing the diversity in attitudes towards sexuality are crucial for developing effective, culturally appropriate sexual health interventions. Interventions must be tailored to the specific cultural context, taking into account the unique norms, values, and attitudes that shape individuals' experiences and pleasure in sexual activities (Institute of Medicine, 2001).

Acknowledging and incorporating cultural differences in attitudes towards sexuality is essential for creating and implementing successful sexual health interventions that respect and address the diverse experiences and expressions of pleasure in various cultural contexts. The role of culture in shaping individuals' attitudes and behaviors concerning sexual health cannot be understated. As we explore the multifaceted impact of culture on sexual health interventions, five key areas must be considered: (1) cultural differences in attitudes towards condom use, (2) cultural variations in attitudes towards sexual communication, (3) cultural disparities in attitudes towards sexual health services, (4) cultural distinctions in the perception of sexual risk, and (5) cultural differences in the emphasis on sexual pleasure. A comprehensive understanding of these complex cultural influences is crucial for developing and implementing sexual health interventions that are both effective and respectful of diverse cultural perspectives and values.

1. <u>Cultural differences in attitudes towards condom use</u>: Cultural norms and values around sexuality can influence individuals' attitudes towards condom use, which can impact the effectiveness of sexual health interventions that promote condom use. For example, some cultures may view condom use as a sign of promiscuity or mistrust, while others may view it as a necessary protection against sexually transmitted infections (Levy et al., 2016).

2. <u>Cultural differences in attitudes towards sexual communication</u>: Cultural attitudes towards sexual contact can also impact the effectiveness of sexual health interventions that promote communication about sexual practices and preferences. For example, some cultures may view discussing sex as taboo or

inappropriate, while others may view it as necessary to maintain a healthy sexual relationship (Herbenick et al., 2018).

3. <u>Cultural differences in attitudes towards sexual health services</u>: Cultural norms and values can also shape individuals' attitudes toward seeking sexual health services, impacting the accessibility and effectiveness of sexual health interventions. For example, some cultures may view seeking sexual health services as stigmatizing or shameful, while others may view it as a responsible and necessary aspect of maintaining sexual health (de Visser et al., 2017).

4. <u>Cultural differences in the perception of sexual risk</u>: Cultural norms and expectations can also shape individuals' perceptions of sexual risk and influence their willingness to engage in safer sexual practices. For example, some cultures may view sexual risk-taking as a source of excitement or pleasure, while others may view it as a source of danger or harm (Zhang et al., 2016).

5. <u>Cultural differences in the emphasis on sexual pleasure</u>: Cultural attitudes towards sexual pleasure can also influence the design and implementation of sexual health interventions, which may need to consider cultural variations in the value placed on sexual pleasure. For example, some cultures may prioritize individual pleasure and sexual exploration, while others may prioritize sexual self-control and restraint (Wight et al., 2016).

Cultural distinctions in attitudes towards food exemplify the diverse approaches to pleasure across societies. In countries like France and Italy, food plays a central role in social life and pleasure, with meals seen as opportunities for enjoyment and fostering connections with others (Bauer & Hamm, 2004). Conversely, some Asian cultures perceive food primarily as a source of sustenance and health, often attributing medicinal properties to traditional foods (Wahlqvist, 2011). Recognizing these variations in cultural perspectives is essential for understanding the multifaceted nature of pleasure in relation to food. Here are five examples of how cultural differences in attitudes toward food can reflect variations in approaches to pleasure:

1. <u>Cultural influences on food preferences</u>: Individual preferences for specific tastes, flavors, and textures are significantly impacted by cultural backgrounds, with some cultures valuing certain flavors over others (Counihan & Van Esterik, 2013).

2. <u>Diverse eating patterns across cultures</u>: Cultural norms and values contribute to differing eating patterns, with some societies emphasizing social contexts for food consumption, while others focus on individual nutritional needs (Mintz & Du Bois, 2002).

3. <u>Symbolic meanings of food in various cultures</u>: Food's cultural significance may reflect underlying values and beliefs, with some societies attributing sacred or special meanings to particular foods, while others view them pragmatically as sources of energy and nutrition (Kittler & Sucher, 2017).

4. <u>Food-related rituals and cultural practices</u>: Pleasurable experiences surrounding food-related rituals, such as holiday feasts or religious ceremonies, are shaped by cultural norms and practices, with specific foods or preparation methods often honoring cultural traditions and beliefs (Sutton, 2001).

5. <u>Varying attitudes towards healthy eating</u>: Cultural attitudes towards health and wellness affect the balance between food enjoyment and healthy eating behaviors, with some cultures prioritizing well-being, while others emphasize the pleasure of food consumption (Jaworowska et al., 2013).

The cultural facet of pleasure, influenced by religious, historical, and traditional factors, plays a significant role in determining how pleasure is experienced and expressed within societies (Csikszentmihalyi & Rochberg-Halton, 1981). For example, certain religious beliefs may view pleasure as an obstacle to spiritual growth, while others might perceive it as an integral aspect of spiritual practice (Csikszentmihalyi & Rochberg-Halton, 1981). Likewise, historical and cultural traditions contribute to the understanding and valuation of pleasure, such as the French "joie de vivre" or the Japanese concept of "wabi-sabi" (Lambert & Brown, 2015). Recognizing these cultural variations is crucial for designing interventions that promote healthy eating behaviors, as strategies should account for diverse cultural values and attitudes towards food and pleasure. Acknowledging the impact of cultural distinctions on approaches to pleasure is vital for developing culturally sensitive and effective interventions to promote health behaviors related to pleasure.

THE ROLE OF PLEASURE IN SOCIETY

The multifaceted nature of pleasure within society manifests itself through its effects on behavior, attitudes, and interpersonal connections. Pleasure can yield positive outcomes such as happiness, bonding, and well-being; however, it may also lead to adverse consequences, including addiction, exploitation, and social disparities. Understanding the significance of pleasure in society is imperative for fostering health, satisfaction, and equity. Thoroughly explored within the realm of social sciences, pleasure represents a complex and nuanced concept intricately connected to individual well-being, social cohesion, and cultural norms.

Here are five examples of the diverse influence of pleasure in society:

1. <u>Pleasure and consumer culture</u>: Pleasure is often linked to consumer culture, with many individuals seeking pleasurable experiences by consuming goods and services. This can lead to excessive consumption, materialism, and environmental degradation (Soper, 2017).

2. <u>Pleasure and social inequality</u>: The availability and accessibility of pleasure can vary widely across different social groups, contributing to social inequality and marginalization. For example, individuals from lower socioeconomic backgrounds may have limited access to pleasurable experiences like travel or cultural events (Wilson & Vanston, 2018).

3. <u>Pleasure and social norms</u>: Social norms and values can shape individuals' experiences and perceptions of pleasure, influencing their behaviors and attitudes towards pleasure-seeking activities. For example, certain forms of pleasure may be stigmatized or taboo in some cultures, while in others, they may be celebrated and valued (Tsai, 2019).

4. <u>Pleasure and technology</u>: Technology has significantly impacted how individuals experience and seek pleasure, with many people relying on digital devices for entertainment and social connection. This can have positive and negative consequences for individuals' well-being and social relationships (Christofides et al., 2009).

5. <u>Pleasure and well-being</u>: Pleasure can be crucial in promoting physical and mental well-being, with pleasurable experiences often linked to increased happiness, reduced stress, and improved health outcomes (Cohen, 2015).

Pleasure's societal role is exemplified through its association with consumption. Consumer goods and services, such as food, drugs, and entertainment, often correlate with pleasure and gratification. However, consumption may also entail negative repercussions, including addiction, financial strain, and environmental harm

(Bourdieu, 1984). Additionally, consumption patterns can unveil social disparities, as certain individuals and groups may possess greater accessibility to pleasurable commodities and experiences (Grunert, 2005).

Here are five examples:

1. <u>Food consumption and pleasure</u>: Pleasure is often associated with food consumption, and people consume food for sustenance and pleasure. This can lead to overeating and obesity, which can have negative health consequences (Flegal et al., 2012).

2. <u>Drug consumption and pleasure</u>: The consumption of drugs is often linked to pleasure, as drugs can alter the brain's chemistry and produce feelings of euphoria. However, drug addiction can negatively affect an individual's physical and mental health and social and economic well-being (National Institute on Drug Abuse, 2021).

3. <u>Entertainment consumption and pleasure</u>: Entertainment products such as movies, music, and video games can provide pleasure and enjoyment to consumers. However, excessive consumption of these products can lead to addiction and social isolation (Ferguson et al., 2017).

4. <u>Travel consumption and pleasure</u>: Travel is often associated with pleasure and adventure, and people tend to consume travel experiences to escape from their daily routines and explore new places. However, excessive travel can have negative environmental consequences, such as greenhouse gas emissions and depletion of natural resources (Gössling et al., 2020).

5. <u>Luxury consumption and pleasure</u>: Luxury goods and experiences are often associated with pleasure and social status. People consume luxury products to signal their social position and distinguish themselves from others. However, luxury consumption can perpetuate social inequalities and contribute to resource depletion and environmental degradation (Bianchi et al., 2018).

Pleasure serves as a crucial element in the formation of social relationships and interactions. It can fortify social connections, enhance intimacy, and bolster overall well-being (Cacioppo et al., 2015). Conversely, pleasure may incite conflict and exploitation, particularly when power imbalances exist (Hochschild, 2012). For example, while sexual pleasure can positively contribute to intimate relationships, it may also be employed as a means of manipulation, coercion, or infliction of harm. Here are five examples that illustrate the impact of pleasure on social relationships:

1. <u>Sexual pleasure and exploitation</u>: Sexual pleasure can play a positive role in intimate relationships, fostering connection and trust. However, it can also be weaponized for manipulation, coercion, or causing harm in cases such as sexual harassment, sexual assault, and human trafficking. Such exploitation highlights the need for awareness and education about consent and healthy sexual relationships (Hawkins, 2020).

2. <u>Pleasure and power dynamics</u>: Unequal power distribution can result in pleasure being used as a tool for conflict and exploitation. For example, the pleasure of domination may drive oppressive and controlling behaviors, as evidenced in workplace bullying and domestic violence. Addressing these power imbalances requires promoting respect, empathy, and equitable treatment in various social contexts (Karpowitz, 2017).

3. <u>Recreational pleasure and social bonding</u>: Engaging in recreational activities like sports, music, and dancing provides opportunities for pleasurable experiences that facilitate social bonding and strengthen social relationships. Shared enjoyment helps to build trust, cooperation, and camaraderie among individuals, fostering a sense of community and belonging (Zhang et al., 2021).

4. <u>Pleasure and addiction</u>: The pursuit of pleasure can sometimes lead to addiction, which can have detrimental effects on social relationships. Addicts may prioritize their addiction over social obligations and relationships, leading to isolation, conflict, and disintegration of personal connections. Addressing addiction requires a comprehensive approach, including support, treatment, and prevention strategies (Friedman et al., 2018).

5. <u>Pleasure and social inequality</u>: The distribution of pleasure can be unequal, with certain individuals or groups enjoying greater access to pleasurable experiences and resources than others. This disparity can contribute to social inequalities and exclusion, perpetuating divisions and marginalization. Efforts to mitigate these disparities should focus on promoting equal access to resources, opportunities, and experiences that foster well-being (Duffy, 2018).

The social dimension of pleasure encompasses the ways in which pleasure is experienced and expressed within various social contexts. Factors such as cultural norms, social class, gender, and ethnicity play a significant role in shaping the types of pleasures individuals seek and value (Jackson, 2016). These factors contribute to the diversity and complexity of pleasure-seeking behaviors, reflecting the multifaceted nature of human experience. Cultural norms surrounding pleasure can differ substantially among societies, illustrating the impact of social factors on pleasure perceptions. In some cultures, pleasure is regarded as an essential and cherished aspect of life, contributing to overall well-being and social cohesion. In these contexts, pleasure-seeking may be encouraged and celebrated as a means of fostering human connection and happiness (Giddens, 2013). Conversely, other cultures may view pleasure as an indication of moral weakness or excess, thereby discouraging indulgence or promoting restraint. These attitudes can shape individuals' understanding of pleasure and influence their pursuit of pleasurable experiences, potentially limiting their access to the benefits associated with positive and healthy pleasure-seeking behaviors (Giddens, 2013). Recognizing the role of social factors in shaping pleasure experiences is crucial for understanding the complexities of human behavior and promoting inclusive and effective interventions that consider diverse cultural perspectives. This awareness can lead to more empathetic and culturally sensitive approaches in addressing challenges related to pleasure-seeking and overall well-being.

Here are five examples that illustrate the social dimension of pleasure:

1. <u>Social class and pleasure</u>: Social class can significantly impact the types of pleasures individuals pursue and their experiences with them. High-status individuals may gravitate towards exclusive and costly pleasures, such as luxury vacations and fine dining, while those from lower social classes might opt for more accessible and affordable pleasures, like community gatherings or picnics (Skeggs, 2005). Understanding the role of social class in pleasure-seeking is vital for developing inclusive interventions that cater to diverse socioeconomic backgrounds.

2. <u>Gender and pleasure</u>: Gender norms can inform the types of pleasures individuals are encouraged to seek and enjoy, often reflecting societal expectations and stereotypes. Men, for example, might be urged to derive pleasure from sports or outdoor activities, while women may be steered towards pleasure through shopping or socializing (Crawford, 1984). Acknowledging the influence of gender norms on pleasure-seeking behaviors is essential for fostering gender-sensitive approaches to health and well-being interventions.

3. <u>Ethnicity and pleasure</u>: Ethnicity can shape the types of pleasures individuals value and pursue. Some ethnic groups may place a higher emphasis on communal and familial pleasures, such as shared meals or cultural celebrations, while others might prioritize individualistic and hedonistic pleasures, like personal achievements or travel (Kivinen, 2011). Recognizing the role of ethnicity in pleasure-seeking allows for a more nuanced understanding of diverse cultural values and practices.

4. <u>Cultural norms and pleasure</u>: Cultural norms can dictate how individuals experience and express pleasure. Some cultures may advocate for self-restraint and moderation in pleasure-seeking, embracing simplicity and balance, while others may encourage the pursuit of intense and exotic pleasures, focusing on novelty and excitement (Kwon, 2011). Appreciating these cultural differences is crucial for designing culturally sensitive interventions that respect diverse values and beliefs.

5. <u>Historical context and pleasure</u>: The historical context in which individuals live can influence the types of pleasures available and valued. Economic and social changes may lead to the emergence of new forms of pleasure, such as the rise of consumer culture or the popularity of digital entertainment, while cultural shifts may bring about changes in the norms around pleasure-seeking, reflecting evolving societal values and expectations (Crossick, 2005). Considering the historical context of pleasure-seeking can provide valuable insights into the dynamic nature of human experiences and inform strategies for promoting well-being across different temporal contexts.

Social class and gender can significantly influence the ways in which pleasure is experienced and expressed, shaping the types and contexts of pleasure individuals seek. For instance, working-class individuals might prioritize tangible, physical pleasures such as food, drink, and sex, whereas middle-class individuals may be more inclined to pursue intellectual or aesthetic pleasures like literature, art, or intellectual debates (Skeggs, 1997). This distinction highlights the complex interplay between social class and cultural capital in shaping pleasure-seeking behaviors. Concurrently, gendered expectations can also contribute to variations in pleasure-seeking and expression. Women may frequently find themselves expected to prioritize the pleasure of others over their own, often adhering to traditional gender roles that emphasize nurturing and caregiving. On the other hand, men may be encouraged to engage in more "masculine" forms of pleasure, such as sports, competition, or assertive displays of power and control (Hochschild, 1983). These gendered norms can perpetuate stereotypes and inequalities, impacting individuals' experiences of pleasure and overall well-being. Understanding the interplay between social class, gender, and pleasure is essential for comprehensively addressing the diverse needs and desires of individuals. By acknowledging these differences, policymakers and practitioners can develop more inclusive and culturally sensitive interventions that foster equitable opportunities for pleasure and well-being across various social and demographic groups.

Here are five examples that illustrate the influence of social class and gender on pleasure:

1. <u>Working-class pleasure</u>: Working-class individuals may gravitate towards physical pleasures, such as eating, drinking, and sex, as a means of coping with daily stressors and the challenges they face. These pleasures can offer a sense of relief, enjoyment, and connection, providing a temporary escape from the demanding aspects of their lives (Skeggs, 1997).

2. <u>Middle-class pleasure</u>: Middle-class individuals often prioritize intellectual and aesthetic pleasures, such as engaging in reading, music, and art. These pursuits not only provide personal satisfaction but also serve to enhance their cultural capital and social status, reflecting their access to resources and opportunities that facilitate cultural consumption (Bourdieu, 1984).

3. <u>Gendered expectations around pleasure</u>: Societal norms often dictate that women prioritize the pleasure of others over their own, reinforcing traditional gender roles centered around caregiving and self-sacrifice. In contrast, men are encouraged to seek out more "masculine" forms of pleasure, such as sports and competition, which perpetuate gender stereotypes and contribute to power imbalances (Hochschild, 1983).

4. <u>Sexual pleasure and gender</u>: Women may encounter more barriers to experiencing sexual pleasure due to cultural taboos, gendered power imbalances, and a lack of comprehensive sexual education. These factors can negatively impact women's sexual satisfaction and overall well-being, exacerbating gender inequalities in the realm of pleasure and intimacy (Braun et al., 2017).

5. <u>Social class and aesthetic pleasure</u>: Middle-class individuals often place greater emphasis on aesthetic pleasures, including art and literature, as a means of

enriching their cultural capital and reinforcing their social status. These pursuits reflect their access to resources, networks, and opportunities that enable them to engage with and appreciate high culture, further distinguishing them from working-class counterparts (Bourdieu, 1984).

Pleasure plays a significant role in shaping work and productivity in society, and its impact can be both positive and negative. Pleasure can motivate individuals to engage in work-related activities and enhance their job satisfaction, leading to greater creativity and innovation (Csikszentmihalyi, 1990). For instance, employees who find pleasure in their work may be more likely to take initiative, develop new ideas and strategies, and perform better on the job. On the other hand, excessive pleasure-seeking may lead to procrastination and decreased productivity, as individuals may prioritize their pleasure over their work obligations (Steel, 2007). Furthermore, pleasure in the workplace can reflect power dynamics, with some individuals having greater access to pleasurable work experiences and rewards than others. For example, individuals in high-status positions may have more opportunities for pleasurable work experiences and rewards, such as autonomy, recognition, and higher salaries, while those in lower-status positions may have limited access to these pleasurable experiences and rewards (Bedeian, 2003). This can lead to social inequalities in the workplace and affect individuals' job satisfaction and well-being. The influence of pleasure on work and productivity is complex, and its impact is shaped by a range of individual and social factors. Understanding the role of pleasure in the workplace can help develop interventions and policies that promote job satisfaction, creativity, and productivity while also addressing social inequalities.

Here are five examples that illustrate the relationship between pleasure and work:

1. <u>Pleasure and creativity</u>: Pleasurable work experiences can enhance creativity and innovation in the workplace, leading to greater job satisfaction and better performance. When employees are encouraged to engage in work that aligns with their passions and interests, they are more likely to become deeply engaged in their tasks, leading to a state of flow that is conducive to creativity (Csikszentmihalyi, 1990). This can result in more innovative solutions, improved productivity, and better overall job satisfaction. However, it is important to note that the relationship between pleasure and creativity is complex and depends on various factors such as the type of work, the level of autonomy, and the individual's personality traits. Moreover, pleasure at work can be enhanced through the creation of a positive work environment that values employee well-being and fosters supportive relationships. This can be achieved through initiatives such as flexible working

hours, wellness programs, and employee recognition programs. When employees feel valued and supported, they are more likely to experience positive emotions, which can enhance their overall well-being and lead to better work outcomes (Eisenberger et al., 2008).

2. <u>Procrastination and pleasure</u>: Pleasurable activities such as browsing social media or watching videos can distract individuals from work, leading to procrastination and decreased productivity. This can be a particular challenge in today's digital age, where there are countless sources of distraction and pleasure readily available. One strategy for combating procrastination is to break down tasks into smaller, more manageable pieces and reward oneself with pleasurable activities after completing each task (Ferrari et al., 1995). This can help individuals stay motivated and on task while still allowing for moments of pleasure throughout the workday. However, it is important to note that not all pleasure is detrimental to work productivity. In fact, taking regular breaks to engage in pleasurable activities can actually enhance productivity and overall well-being. This is because breaks can help to reduce stress and prevent burnout, leading to greater focus and motivation when returning to work (Sonnentag & Fritz, 2007). Therefore, it is essential to strike a balance between pleasure and work, ensuring that pleasurable activities are both enjoyable and conducive to work productivity.

3. <u>Power dynamics and pleasure</u>: Workplace power imbalances can affect who has access to pleasurable work experiences and rewards, leading to social inequalities and dissatisfaction. This can be particularly challenging in hierarchical organizations where power is concentrated in the hands of a few individuals. In these settings, those with less power may have limited access to pleasurable work experiences and may be more likely to experience negative emotions such as frustration and dissatisfaction (Bedeian, 2003). To address this issue, it is essential to create a more egalitarian workplace culture that values diversity, equity, and inclusion. This can be achieved through initiatives such as mentorship programs, diversity and inclusion training, and transparent communication channels. Moreover, leaders who prioritize employee well-being and seek to create a positive work environment can help to mitigate the negative effects of power imbalances on pleasure. This can be achieved through initiatives such as promoting work-life balance, providing opportunities for skill development, and creating a culture of open communication and collaboration. By valuing employee well-being and prioritizing positive work experiences for all individuals, leaders can help to create a more equitable and satisfying workplace culture.

4. <u>Motivation and pleasure</u>: Pleasurable work experiences can enhance motivation and engagement, leading to better performance and job satisfaction. When individuals experience pleasure at work, they are more likely to become deeply engaged in their tasks and experience a state of flow that is conducive to motivation and productivity (Csikszentmihalyi, 1990). This can result in better performance outcomes, increased job satisfaction, and improved overall well-being.

5. <u>Power dynamics and pleasure</u>: Power dynamics in the workplace can also have a significant impact on employees' experiences of pleasure. Those in higher positions of power may have more control over how pleasurable work experiences are distributed, which can lead to social inequalities and dissatisfaction. Research shows that those in lower positions of power, such as women and people of color, are more likely to experience work environments that are less pleasurable than their higher-status colleagues (McGregor et al., 2018). Moreover, those in higher positions may also have more access to rewards that are associated with pleasurable work experiences, such as promotions or bonuses, further exacerbating these social inequalities. To address this issue, organizations can implement policies and practices that promote equal access to pleasurable work experiences and rewards. For example, diversity and inclusion programs can help address power imbalances in the workplace, allowing employees of all backgrounds to feel valued and included. Additionally, flexible work arrangements can help employees balance their work and personal lives, allowing them to engage in pleasurable activities outside of work, which can contribute to overall well-being.

6. <u>Motivation and pleasure</u>: Pleasurable work experiences can also enhance motivation and engagement, leading to better performance and job satisfaction. Pleasurable experiences can increase employees' sense of autonomy and control over their work, leading to a greater sense of investment in their work outcomes (Deci et al., 1999). Additionally, pleasurable experiences can increase employees' sense of competence and mastery, leading to greater confidence in their abilities to perform their work tasks. To promote pleasurable work experiences that enhance motivation, organizations can provide opportunities for employee autonomy and creativity. For example, allowing employees to work on projects that align with their interests or providing opportunities for self-directed learning can promote a sense of autonomy and control. Additionally, organizations can provide recognition and feedback for employees' work, which can promote a sense of competence and mastery.

7. <u>Burnout and pleasure</u>: Excessive work demands, and stress can lead to burnout, diminishing work enjoyment, productivity, and job satisfaction. Burnout is a state of emotional, physical, and mental exhaustion that can result from prolonged exposure to work-related stressors (Maslach et al., 2001). Burnout can lead to decreased engagement in work, reduced motivation, and increased absenteeism and turnover. To prevent burnout and promote pleasurable work experiences, organizations can implement practices that promote work-life balance and reduce work-related stressors. This can include providing opportunities for flexible work arrangements, such as telecommuting or job sharing, as well as promoting self-care and stress management strategies, such as mindfulness or exercise programs. Additionally, organizations can provide resources and support for employees experiencing burnout, such as employee assistance programs or counseling services.

Pleasure is not only a reflection of personal preferences and attitudes but also a product of cultural and social norms. For example, cultural norms may dictate what is considered pleasurable, such as certain foods, drinks, or activities, and how they should be enjoyed. Cultural attitudes towards pleasure can also be influenced by historical and political contexts, which may affect the types of pleasure that are acceptable or encouraged in society. Moreover, the distribution of pleasure and access to pleasurable experiences can reflect power dynamics and social inequalities, with certain individuals and groups having greater opportunities for pleasurable experiences than others. The relationship between pleasure and attitudes can also have implications for social change. For instance, promoting pleasurable experiences that align with pro-social values, such as generosity and compassion, can lead to a more empathetic and caring society. On the other hand, promoting pleasurable experiences that prioritize individualistic and materialistic values can lead to a more self-centered and consumerist society. Thus, understanding the role of pleasure in shaping attitudes and values is critical for promoting social norms that align with positive social outcomes, such as social justice, equality, and sustainability.

Here are ten examples that illustrate the role of pleasure in shaping attitudes and values:

1. <u>Advertising and materialism</u>: Pleasure is often used as a marketing tool to promote materialistic values and encourage the consumption of goods and services. Advertisers rely on the allure of pleasure to create a desire for products and to make consumers feel that they are missing out on something

if they do not purchase them. This can lead to a vicious cycle of consumption, where individuals are constantly seeking pleasure through material possessions, leading to debt and financial insecurity (Kasser, 2002). On the other hand, pleasure can also be used as a tool to promote sustainable consumption and ethical values, by emphasizing the pleasures of simplicity, community, and environmental consciousness (Caruana & Ewing, 2010).

2. <u>Media and violence</u>: Pleasure can be derived from media that glorify violence, leading to desensitization and normalization of violent behavior. Exposure to violent media can lead to aggressive attitudes and behaviors, desensitization to violence, and decreased empathy for victims of violence (Anderson et al., 2003). However, pleasure can also be derived from media that promote positive values and behaviors, such as empathy, social responsibility, and cultural diversity. Media can be used as a powerful tool to shape attitudes and behaviors, promoting positive social norms and values (Van der Voort et al., 2018).

3. <u>Environmentalism and pleasure</u>: Pleasure can be used to promote environmentalism by emphasizing the joys of being in nature and connecting with the natural world. Environmental educators and activists can use pleasure to motivate individuals to engage in pro-environmental behaviors, such as reducing energy consumption, promoting sustainable transportation, and protecting wildlife habitats (Kahn, 1999). However, pleasure can also lead to unsustainable behaviors, such as recreational activities that damage natural habitats, overconsumption of resources, and waste generation. Thus, it is crucial to promote a balanced approach to pleasure and environmental sustainability, where pleasure is derived from sustainable and ethical practices (Steg & Vlek, 2009).

4. <u>Social justice and pleasure</u>: Pleasure can be used to promote social justice by emphasizing the positive emotions that come from helping others and contributing to society. Pleasure can be derived from engaging in social justice work, such as volunteering, activism, and community building, leading to a sense of purpose and well-being (Post, 2005). However, pleasure can also be derived from maintaining social hierarchies and reinforcing social inequalities, such as through discrimination, prejudice, and exploitation. It is essential to promote a social justice framework that values pleasure as a tool for promoting equality and well-being for all individuals, rather than just for the privileged few (Pettigrew & Meertens, 1995).

5. <u>Education and pleasure</u>: Pleasure can promote lifelong learning by emphasizing the joy of acquiring new knowledge and skills. Pleasurable learning experiences can enhance motivation, engagement, and academic achievement, leading to positive academic outcomes and personal growth (Csikszentmihalyi & Csikszentmihalyi, 1988). However, pleasure can also lead to a superficial approach to learning, where individuals prioritize pleasurable experiences over deep learning and critical thinking. It is crucial to promote a balanced approach to pleasure and education, where pleasure is derived from meaningful and challenging learning experiences that promote personal growth and academic achievement (Hidi & Renninger, 2006).

Pleasure is a multifaceted and complex concept that has a significant impact on social interaction, cultural norms, and individual well-being. Social and cultural dimensions of pleasure are interdependent, with social factors such as culture, social class, gender, and ethnicity influencing the way people experience and express pleasure, and cultural factors such as religion, history, and tradition shaping how people understand and value pleasure within their respective cultural contexts. It is essential to investigate the dynamic relationship between pleasure and social and cultural factors and to develop strategies to promote healthy and satisfying forms of pleasure within different societies.

<u>Reflective questions for readers:</u>

1. How do social and cultural factors influence the way people experience pleasure in their daily lives?
2. What are some of the cultural differences in the way pleasure is valued and expressed across societies and how do these differences impact the well-being of individuals within those societies?
3. How can we promote healthy and satisfying forms of pleasure in society while acknowledging and respecting cultural diversity?
4. In what ways can an understanding of the social and cultural dimensions of pleasure contribute to the development of policies and practices that enhance individual and collective well-being?
5. How can we balance the pursuit of pleasure with the need to consider the broader social and environmental consequences of our actions?

<u>PLEASURE AND SOCIAL NORMS</u>

At its core, pleasure is an essential element of human experience, serving as a driving force behind motivation and behavior (Kringelbach & Berridge, 2010). The experience of pleasure is closely linked to the release of dopamine, a neurotransmitter that plays a critical role in the brain's reward and motivation systems (Berridge & Kringelbach, 2015). As such, pleasure has long been a topic of interest in psychology, with many studies exploring how it shapes behavior and influences decision-making. Some theories of motivation propose that individuals are primarily motivated by the pursuit of pleasure and the avoidance of pain, highlighting the central role of pleasure in shaping human behavior (Fishbein & Ajzen, 2010). Moreover, the experience and pursuit of pleasure are influenced by a range of individual and contextual factors, including genetics, culture, and social norms (Knobloch-Westerwick & Meng, 2009). Social norms, in particular, play a significant role in shaping the types of pleasures individuals seek and how they express them. Conforming to social norms regarding the expression of pleasure can lead to social approval, while violating these norms can result in social stigma and punishment. Understanding the role of social norms in shaping the pursuit and experience of pleasure can help inform interventions to promote healthy and fulfilling forms of pleasure within diverse societies.

Reflective questions:
1. How does your culture or society view pleasure, and how has this influenced your pursuit of pleasure?
2. How do individual factors, such as genetics and personality, influence how you experience pleasure?
3. What are some potential drawbacks of pursuing pleasure, and how can these be balanced with the benefits?
4. How might social norms around pleasure differ across cultures, and how can we respect and navigate these differences?
5. In what ways can we promote healthy and fulfilling forms of pleasure within our communities and societies?

Here are ten examples of social norms:

1. <u>Gender Norms</u>: Gender norms refer to social expectations regarding behavior, dress, and attitudes for individuals based on their gender. Such norms differ among cultures and can have a significant impact on an individual's life, shaping their self-expression and choices. Gender norms can influence how people interact, form relationships, and participate in society. They can also lead to gender inequality and discrimination. Addressing and challenging gender norms is essential for promoting gender equality and creating a more

inclusive society.

2. <u>Manners</u>: Manners refer to a set of social norms that dictate appropriate behavior in different settings. These norms vary across cultures and are taught from an early age. They can include behaviors such as greeting others, table manners, and displaying emotions. Manners play a crucial role in social interactions, as they help individuals navigate social situations and show respect to others. However, they can also create barriers to communication and perpetuate social inequalities based on social class or cultural background.

3. <u>Political Correctness</u>: Political correctness refers to social norms that regulate language and behavior to promote sensitivity and respect for marginalized groups. These norms aim to reduce discrimination and prejudice and create a more inclusive society. They can include guidelines for the use of language and avoiding language or behaviors that are offensive or disrespectful. However, debates around political correctness also raise questions about freedom of speech and the extent to which individuals should be held accountable for their language and behavior.

4. <u>Personal Space</u>: Personal space refers to the physical distance that individuals maintain from others during social interactions. Different cultures have different norms regarding personal space, with some cultures valuing close physical contact while others preferring a more significant distance. Personal space norms can affect communication, as individuals may feel uncomfortable if their personal space is invaded. They can also affect relationships, with different norms for physical touch and affection among family members, friends, and romantic partners.

5. <u>Gift-Giving</u>: Gift-giving is a social norm that varies across cultures and can involve different expectations around the types of gifts given, when they should be given, and how they should be wrapped. Gift-giving can have a significant social and economic impact, with some cultures valuing extravagant gifts as a sign of status and others preferring more practical or thoughtful gifts. Gift-giving norms can also affect interpersonal relationships and social hierarchies.

6. <u>Religion</u>: Religion refers to a set of beliefs and practices that dictate behaviors and attitudes related to the divine or supernatural. Different religions have different norms regarding dress, behavior, and morality. Religious norms can have a significant impact on an individual's life, shaping their values, beliefs,

and social interactions. However, religious norms can also create conflict and intolerance between different groups.

7. <u>Social Hierarchies</u>: Social hierarchies refer to social norms that dictate appropriate behaviors and attitudes related to power and status. Social hierarchies can be based on various factors, such as age, gender, race, social class, or occupation. Social hierarchies can affect social interactions, with individuals expected to show deference to those in positions of authority or higher status. However, social hierarchies can also perpetuate inequality and discrimination.

8. <u>Dress Codes</u>: Dress codes refer to social norms that dictate appropriate attire for different contexts, such as formal events or workplaces. Dress codes can vary across cultures and can be influenced by factors such as climate, social class, or religion. Dress codes can affect an individual's self-expression and create barriers to social mobility or inclusion.

9. <u>Dating and Courtship</u>: Dating and courtship refer to social norms that dictate appropriate behaviors related to romantic relationships. Different cultures have different norms around dating and courtship, with some valuing traditional gender roles and others promoting more egalitarian relationships. Dating and courtship norms can affect social interactions and have a significant impact on an individual's social and emotional well-being.

10. <u>Use of Technology</u>: Use of technology refers to social norms that dictate appropriate behaviors and etiquette related to using devices, such as phones or computers, in public and private spaces. Technology use norms can include guidelines for smartphone use during social interactions or expectations around social media posting. They can affect communication, relationships, and privacy. As technology use becomes more integrated into daily life, these norms are constantly evolving and shaping our social interactions and behaviors. It is essential to consider the impact of technology use norms on individuals and society as a whole.

The interplay between pleasure and social norms is a complex and dynamic relationship that shapes individual behavior and social interactions. Pleasure is a subjective experience that is influenced by cultural, social, and personal factors. Social norms guide individuals' behaviors, influencing the types of pleasures they seek and how they express them. This relationship can be both explicit and implicit, with social norms shaping acceptable behaviors and attitudes towards pleasure. For example, in some cultures, pleasure may be celebrated and encouraged, while in others, it may be stigmatized and discouraged. Furthermore, social norms regarding pleasure can change over time, reflecting evolving attitudes and values. The legalization of marijuana and the increasing acceptance of non-traditional sexual relationships are examples of changing social norms that impact how individuals experience pleasure. These changes may also result in the normalization of previously stigmatized behaviors, such as non-monogamous relationships or BDSM. Thus, the relationship between pleasure and social norms is not static, but rather a dynamic and evolving process.

<u>Reflective questions for readers</u>:

1. How have social norms influenced your pursuit of pleasure in your personal life?
2. How have changing social norms impacted your experience of pleasure?
3. In what ways have social norms impacted how you express pleasure in different contexts?
4. How do social norms vary across different cultures and communities, and how do they shape attitudes towards pleasure?
5. In what ways can individuals challenge or subvert social norms regarding pleasure, and what are the potential consequences of doing so?

The relationship between pleasure and social norms is a complex and multifaceted process that has garnered significant attention in various fields, including psychology, sociology, and cultural studies. Pleasure is a subjective experience that is influenced by various factors, including cultural and social norms, individual values, and personal history. Social norms refer to the unwritten rules and expectations that guide individuals' behaviors in social situations. These norms provide a framework for social interactions and shape the types of pleasures that are acceptable in a given culture or community. The influence of social norms on pleasure-seeking behaviors and experiences has been the subject of considerable research, highlighting the intricate interplay between the two phenomena. For instance, some social norms discourage specific pleasurable behaviors, such as drug use or promiscuous sexual behavior, while others encourage certain types of pleasurable experiences, such as participating in social events or pursuing hobbies and interests. Social norms can also impact how individuals express pleasure and the contexts in which they are allowed to do so. The expression of pleasure can be shaped by cultural, social, and personal factors, with social norms acting as a powerful influence on this aspect of pleasure. However, the relationship between pleasure and social norms is also context-dependent, with the types of pleasures and social norms varying widely across cultures and communities. For example, some cultures encourage open expressions of pleasure, while others view such expressions as inappropriate or even shameful. The relationship between pleasure and social norms is further complicated by changing social attitudes and values. Societal changes, such as the increasing acceptance of non-traditional sexual relationships or the legalization of recreational drugs, can lead to shifts in social norms that, in turn, influence how individuals experience and express pleasure. Further research is needed to fully understand the complex relationship between pleasure and social norms. The examination of this relationship requires interdisciplinary approaches that consider cultural, social, and personal factors that influence the experience and expression of pleasure. The study of this relationship has implications for various fields, including public health, sociology, psychology, and cultural studies. Understanding how social norms shape our experiences of pleasure and how these experiences contribute to broader social structures and cultural norms can inform interventions aimed at promoting healthy and positive pleasure-seeking behaviors and contribute to a more nuanced understanding of the complex relationship between pleasure and social norms.

Reflective Questions:

1. How do cultural norms and values shape our understanding and pursuit of pleasure within different societies? Can you identify any specific cultural influences that have impacted your own experiences and perceptions of pleasure?

2. In what ways do various cultures emphasize or downplay the importance of pleasure in their belief systems, rituals, and daily practices? Are there specific cultural examples that challenge your preconceptions about pleasure and its role in human life?

3. How can exposure to diverse cultural perspectives on pleasure broaden our understanding of what constitutes a pleasurable experience and enrich our own pursuit of happiness? In what ways might engaging with other cultures' views on pleasure inspire us to reevaluate our own beliefs and values?

4. How do cultural expressions of pleasure, such as art, music, cuisine, and celebrations, reflect the unique values and experiences of a specific society? How can engaging with these expressions help us develop a deeper appreciation for the cultural dimensions of pleasure?

5. In our interconnected world, how might cross-cultural exchanges impact our shared pursuit of pleasure? What opportunities and challenges arise from exploring the relationship between cultural perspectives on pleasure and our personal beliefs and experiences?

(See "7" in the reference section for all references.)

DARK SIDE OF PLEASURE

The concept of the "dark side of pleasure" refers to the negative outcomes associated with engaging in pleasurable activities. These adverse consequences may manifest themselves in the form of physical, psychological, or social harm, and can be particularly concerning when the pleasurable activity leads to addiction. For example, excessive alcohol consumption, gambling, and drug use can bring immediate pleasure but may lead to addiction, financial problems, and health issues. These consequences can occur due to the overstimulation of the brain's reward system, which leads individuals to seek out these pleasurable experiences even when the cost outweighs the benefits. In psychology, the dark side of pleasure is often linked to the concept of hedonic adaptation, which refers to the idea that individuals quickly become accustomed to and habituated to pleasurable experiences. This can lead to the pursuit of more intense or extreme forms of pleasure in order to maintain the same level of enjoyment. Over time, this can result in a vicious cycle of seeking pleasure, experiencing diminishing returns, and eventually experiencing negative consequences. Furthermore, the dark side of pleasure can have social implications as well. For instance, indulging in certain pleasurable activities may lead to social isolation or exclusion, which can result in further negative consequences for an individual's mental health. Understanding the dark side of pleasure is crucial for promoting healthy behavior and preventing addiction and other negative outcomes. By recognizing the potential negative consequences associated with pleasurable activities, individuals can make more informed choices and take steps to mitigate any risks.

ADDICTION AND PLEASURE

The concepts of addiction and pleasure are intricately intertwined when it comes to discussions of substance use and other problematic behaviors. Addiction is characterized by persistent and compulsive engagement in a behavior despite its adverse consequences, while pleasure is a significant driver of this behavior. Pleasure is a multifaceted and multidimensional experience that various stimuli, including drugs, food, sex, and other rewards, can elicit. When encountered, these rewards activate the brain's reward system, which regulates feelings of pleasure and motivation. This system comprises several brain regions, including the ventral tegmental area, the nucleus accumbens, and the prefrontal cortex. Drugs of abuse, such as alcohol, opioids, and cocaine, can hijack this reward system by causing a rapid and intense dopamine release. Dopamine is a neurotransmitter associated with feelings of pleasure and reward. With repeated drug use, changes in the brain occur that increase the risk of addiction, such as alterations in dopamine signaling, changes in gene expression, and reductions in the number of dopamine receptors. The relationship between pleasure and addiction is complex, and addiction can both enhance and undermine pleasure. On the one hand, individuals with addiction often report that their drug of choice provides them with pleasure, and this pleasure is one of the key reasons they continue to use it. On the other hand, addiction can reduce the overall capacity for pleasure by desensitizing the brain's reward system and leading to a decrease in the number of dopamine receptors. This can create a vicious cycle in which individuals with addiction must use larger and larger amounts of their drug of choice to experience the same level of pleasure. Moreover, addiction can also affect other areas of the brain, including the prefrontal cortex, which is involved in decision-making and impulse control. These changes can further impair an individual's ability to resist the urge to engage in the addictive behavior, even in the face of adverse consequences. It is essential to understand the complex interplay between addiction and pleasure, as it can inform the development of effective interventions to prevent and treat addiction. Targeting the brain's reward system and cognitive processes involved in addiction could be crucial in developing new therapeutic approaches for addiction.

THE DOWNSIDE OF SEEKING PLEASURE

Pleasure-seeking behavior is defined as the pursuit of activities or experiences that are pleasurable or enjoyable. Although seeking pleasure can have many positive benefits, such as increasing happiness and reducing stress, it can also have negative consequences, including the potential for addiction. Addiction is a complex disorder characterized by persistent and compulsive engagement in a behavior despite adverse consequences, and pleasure is often a key driver of this behavior.Pleasurable activities such as drug use, gambling, and excessive internet use can trigger the release of dopamine, a neurotransmitter associated with pleasure and reward. Over time, the brain may become dependent on these pleasurable experiences, leading to addiction and compulsive behavior. The brain's reward system, consisting of several brain regions, including the ventral tegmental area, the nucleus accumbens, and the prefrontal cortex, plays a crucial role in addiction.Addiction can seriously impact an individual's health, relationships, and financial stability. For instance, drug addiction can lead to physical health problems, such as liver damage or overdose, and strain relationships with family and friends. Furthermore, addiction can negatively affect an individual's motivation and productivity. Overly focusing on seeking pleasure can lead to neglecting other important responsibilities and activities, reducing one's incentive to work or study, and negatively impacting their future opportunities and success. In addition, pleasure-seeking can also lead to financial problems. Engaging in gambling or excessive shopping can lead to debt and financial stress, which can cause additional stress and impact an individual's mental health. It is essential to recognize the potential downsides of pleasure-seeking behavior to prevent addiction and its negative consequences. Effective interventions to prevent and treat addiction include targeting the brain's reward system and cognitive processes involved in addiction. Such approaches can help to reduce the motivation to engage in addictive behaviors, improve decision-making, and enhance impulse control. Education and awareness of the potential negative consequences of pleasure-seeking behavior can also be beneficial in promoting healthy choices and preventing addiction. Understanding the complex interplay between pleasure-seeking and addiction can inform the development of new therapeutic approaches for addiction treatment and prevention.

In the pursuit of pleasure, individuals may experience a lack of fulfillment and dissatisfaction, which can negatively impact their mental health and well-being. Although seeking pleasure is a natural human tendency, it is important to recognize its potential downsides. Addiction, decreased motivation, financial problems, and a lack of fulfillment are some of the negative consequences associated with an overemphasis on pleasure-seeking. While the release of dopamine and serotonin in the brain is linked to pleasurable experiences and feelings of happiness, the constant pursuit of pleasure can adversely affect an individual's emotional, physical, and mental health.

One of the major downsides of seeking pleasure is the risk of addiction, where an individual becomes reliant on pleasurable activities to maintain their well-being. This can lead to a vicious cycle where the individual seeks more intense experiences to achieve the same level of satisfaction, ultimately resulting in destructive behaviors. Another downside is hedonic adaptation, whereby individuals become accustomed to a certain level of pleasure, resulting in a reduced response to the same stimuli over time. This can lead to a never-ending search for new and more intense sources of pleasure that may not necessarily lead to increased happiness or well-being. This paper will explore the negative impact of seeking pleasure, focusing on addiction, hedonic adaptation, and its effect on personal relationships.

In addition to its potential adverse effects on mental health, the pursuit of pleasure can also negatively impact personal relationships. A preoccupation with pleasure-seeking may result in self-centeredness and a lack of empathy towards others. This can strain relationships, as the individual prioritizes their own gratification over the needs and emotions of others (Twenge & Campbell, 2009). While seeking pleasure is a natural human instinct, it is crucial to maintain a balance between pleasure-seeking and other aspects of life, such as personal growth, social connections, and long-term well-being. Overemphasizing pleasure-seeking can lead to addiction, hedonic adaptation, and harmful effects on personal relationships. It is, therefore, essential for individuals to be mindful of the potential downsides of excessive pleasure-seeking and work towards achieving a balance between their personal gratification and the needs and emotions of those around them. By cultivating empathy, social connection, and personal growth, individuals can enjoy pleasurable experiences without compromising their overall well-being and the quality of their relationships.

Reflective questions for readers:

1. Have you ever experienced a negative impact on your personal relationships due to your pursuit of pleasure? If so, how did it affect your relationships?
2. How do you balance your pursuit of pleasure with other aspects of your life, such as personal growth and social connections?
3. Have you ever witnessed someone close to you prioritize their own pleasure-seeking over the needs and emotions of others? How did it affect your relationship with them?
4. In what ways can excessive pleasure-seeking lead to addiction and hedonic adaptation? How can you prevent these negative outcomes?
5. How can cultivating empathy, social connection, and personal growth enhance your overall well-being and the quality of your relationships while still allowing you to enjoy pleasurable experiences?

THE CONSEQUENCES OF AN EXCESSIVE PURSUIT OF PLEASURE

Hedonism, as an excessive pursuit of pleasure, represents a lifestyle that emphasizes the acquisition of pleasure while avoiding pain. While pleasure-seeking is a natural part of human life, excessive hedonism can lead to negative consequences that can affect one's physical, emotional, and mental health. The negative outcomes of excessive pleasure-seeking can arise from an individual's preoccupation with pleasure and the avoidance of discomfort or pain. Such an approach to life can lead to an unbalanced lifestyle that neglects other important aspects of life, such as personal growth, social connection, and long-term well-being. Excessive pleasure-seeking can lead to addiction, a state where an individual becomes heavily reliant on pleasurable experiences to achieve a sense of well-being. Addiction can take various forms, including substance abuse, compulsive gambling, or overeating, among others. The constant pursuit of pleasure can also lead to hedonic adaptation, whereby an individual becomes desensitized to pleasurable experiences, and their enjoyment of those experiences diminishes over time. This can result in individuals seeking out new and more intense sources of pleasure, which may lead to destructive behaviors and further emotional detachment.

Furthermore, the excessive pursuit of pleasure can negatively impact personal relationships. A preoccupation with pleasure-seeking can lead to a self-centered lifestyle that lacks empathy for others. Such individuals prioritize their own pleasure and gratification over the needs and emotions of others, which can result in strained relationships. A hedonistic lifestyle can also lead to social isolation, as individuals may neglect their social connections and become increasingly focused on their pleasure-seeking activities. To mitigate the negative outcomes of excessive pleasure-seeking, individuals can adopt a balanced approach that integrates pleasure-seeking with other important aspects of life. This approach involves cultivating empathy and social connection while focusing on personal growth and long-term well-being. In doing so, individuals can enjoy pleasurable experiences while avoiding the negative outcomes of hedonism.

<u>Physical health consequences</u>: The excessive pursuit of pleasure, particularly through substance use, can result in detrimental physical health consequences. Alcohol and drug abuse, in particular, can cause addiction, liver damage, and cardiovascular disease, which can lead to life-threatening complications. According to the National Institute on Drug Abuse (2018), drug abuse can cause a range of health issues, including heart disease, lung disease, and chronic liver disease. Additionally, excessive drinking can cause alcohol poisoning, which can result in severe health complications, such as brain damage, coma, and even death. Apart from addiction and chronic illnesses, excessive pleasure-seeking behaviors, such as drug and alcohol abuse, can lead to reckless and dangerous behaviors. Engaging in such behaviors can result in accidents and injuries that can be life-threatening. For instance, drunk driving is a leading cause of fatal accidents, which not only puts the life of the driver at risk but also endangers the lives of others on the road (Center for Substance Abuse Research, 2016). Similarly, drug abuse can impair an individual's judgment, leading to risky behaviors that can result in injury or harm to oneself or others. It is crucial to understand that the pursuit of pleasure, particularly through substance use, can have significant consequences on physical health. It is essential to adopt a balanced approach that prioritizes health and safety while still allowing for pleasurable experiences. Adopting healthy habits, such as regular exercise, a balanced diet, and stress-reduction techniques, can improve physical health and reduce the negative effects of excessive pleasure-seeking behaviors. Moreover, seeking professional help and support groups can be beneficial in treating addiction and other health complications resulting from excessive pleasure-seeking.

<u>Mental health consequences</u>: The excessive pursuit of pleasure can have significant effects on an individual's mental health. Constantly seeking pleasure and avoiding discomfort can result in anxiety, depression, and feelings of emptiness. According to

Baumeister and Tierney (2011), hedonic pursuits, when taken to extremes, can lead to a lack of purpose and meaning in life, which can contribute to a sense of dissatisfaction and decreased mental well-being. Furthermore, individuals who engage in excessive pleasure-seeking behaviors, such as substance abuse, are at a higher risk of developing mood and anxiety disorders. The National Institute on Mental Health (2019) reports that individuals who misuse drugs or alcohol are more likely to experience symptoms of depression and anxiety. This can be attributed to the chemical imbalances that arise from substance abuse, which can cause alterations in the brain's reward and pleasure systems, leading to long-term changes in mood and behavior. The impact of excessive pleasure-seeking on mental health can also extend to an individual's social and professional life. Hedonic pursuits can lead to social isolation, as individuals may prioritize their own pleasure-seeking activities over maintaining social connections. This can result in a lack of emotional support and a decreased sense of belonging, leading to increased feelings of loneliness and depression. Additionally, the excessive pursuit of pleasure can negatively impact an individual's professional life, resulting in decreased productivity, decreased motivation, and impaired decision-making abilities. To mitigate the negative impact of excessive pleasure-seeking on mental health, individuals can adopt a more balanced approach that prioritizes overall well-being. This involves focusing on activities that promote personal growth, social connections, and positive emotions, in addition to pleasurable experiences. Incorporating mindfulness practices, such as meditation and yoga, can also help individuals develop a more balanced perspective on pleasure-seeking and avoid the negative effects on mental health. Seeking professional help, such as therapy or counseling, can also be beneficial for individuals struggling with addiction or mental health issues resulting from excessive pleasure-seeking behaviors.

<u>Social consequences</u>: Excessive pleasure-seeking can also have significant social consequences. When individuals prioritize pleasure above other aspects of their lives, such as work or relationships, they may struggle to maintain healthy and meaningful connections. This can result in social isolation, reduced emotional support, and a decreased sense of belonging. Kasser and Ryan (1996) argue that individuals who prioritize hedonic pursuits may prioritize their own interests over their relationships, leading to strained relationships and diminished social capital. Engaging in excessive and dangerous pleasure-seeking behaviors, such as substance use, can further exacerbate social problems. Substance abuse can impair judgment and behavior, leading to risky and dangerous behaviors that can put oneself and others in danger. For instance, individuals who engage in drug use may become socially isolated as they withdraw from social relationships to indulge in their hedonic pursuits. This can lead to strained relationships and a reduced sense of social support, exacerbating the negative effects on mental health. To mitigate the social consequences

of excessive pleasure-seeking, individuals can adopt a more balanced approach that prioritizes social connections and meaningful relationships. This involves investing time and effort in building and maintaining social connections, engaging in activities that promote social interaction and emotional support. Additionally, individuals can seek out professional help, such as therapy or counseling, to address issues related to substance abuse and addiction that may be affecting their social relationships. By developing a more balanced perspective on pleasure-seeking, individuals can enjoy pleasurable experiences while maintaining meaningful connections and improving their overall well-being.

<u>Financial consequences</u>: The pursuit of pleasure can have significant economic consequences, particularly when individuals engage in excessive pleasure-seeking behaviors, such as drugs, gambling, or excessive shopping. According to the American Psychological Association (2018), individuals who engage in these behaviors may spend large amounts of money, leading to financial instability and debt. This can significantly impact an individual's overall well-being, leading to increased stress and anxiety. Excessive pleasure-seeking can result in a lack of financial responsibility, leading to the accumulation of debt and reduced financial security. Kasser and Ryan (1996) argue that individuals who prioritize hedonic pursuits may engage in impulsive spending, leading to financial instability and the accumulation of debt. This can exacerbate the negative impact on mental health, leading to stress, anxiety, and reduced overall well-being. Additionally, the economic consequences of excessive pleasure-seeking can extend to an individual's professional life. Engaging in excessive pleasure-seeking behaviors can result in decreased productivity and motivation, leading to decreased job performance and reduced earning potential. This can further exacerbate financial instability, leading to a range of negative consequences, including reduced access to healthcare, increased stress levels, and decreased social status. To mitigate the economic consequences of excessive pleasure-seeking, individuals can adopt a more balanced approach that prioritizes financial responsibility and long-term well-being. This involves developing a budget and sticking to it, avoiding impulsive spending, and seeking out professional help to address any financial problems resulting from excessive pleasure-seeking behaviors. By adopting a more balanced approach, individuals can reduce the negative impact of excessive pleasure-seeking on their economic and overall well-being.

QUICK REVIEW

The excessive pursuit of pleasure can have many negative consequences, which can be categorized into several broad categories including physical health, mental health, social and relationship difficulties, and financial instability. Physical health consequences may include addiction, liver damage, and cardiovascular disease resulting from substance abuse, as well as injuries from engaging in reckless and dangerous behaviors associated with hedonism. Chronic substance abuse can also impair the immune system, leading to an increased risk of infectious diseases and other health complications. Mental health problems are also common among those who engage in excessive pleasure-seeking behaviors. The pursuit of pleasure and avoidance of pain can lead to a sense of emptiness, anxiety, depression, and an overall lack of purpose or meaning in life. In addition, substance abuse is often associated with the development of mood and anxiety disorders. Social and relationship difficulties are also common among those who prioritize hedonistic pursuits. Excessive pleasure-seeking behaviors may result in social isolation, strained relationships, and a lack of emotional support. The pursuit of pleasure may lead to a self-centered lifestyle that neglects the needs and emotions of others, leading to a lack of social capital and difficulty maintaining healthy relationships. Financial instability is another negative consequence of excessive pleasure-seeking behaviors. Engaging in behaviors such as drug use, gambling, or excessive shopping may lead to impulsive spending and debt accumulation. This can lead to significant financial stress and anxiety, as well as reduced access to healthcare, decreased social status, and other economic consequences. Balancing pleasure and other aspects of life is essential to avoid these negative outcomes. Individuals must prioritize their overall well-being, including physical and mental health, social connections, and financial stability, in addition to their desire for pleasure. By adopting a more balanced approach, individuals can reduce the negative impact of excessive pleasure-seeking on their overall well-being and improve their quality of life. This may involve seeking professional help, developing healthy habits, and engaging in activities that promote personal growth and social connection.

Reflective Questions for readers:

1. How do you define the "dark side" of pleasure, and in what ways have you encountered or experienced this aspect of pleasure in your own life? Can you identify specific instances or situations that have revealed the potential dangers or negative consequences associated with the pursuit of pleasure?

2. Reflect on the role of moderation and balance in the pursuit of pleasure. How can an awareness of the dark side of pleasure help guide us in making more mindful and responsible choices when seeking pleasurable experiences?

3. In what ways can societal norms, expectations, and pressures contribute to the

dark side of pleasure, such as encouraging excessive indulgence, addiction, or harmful behaviors? How might we challenge these influences and cultivate a healthier relationship with pleasure?

4. How do various philosophical, spiritual, or psychological frameworks address the dark side of pleasure, and what guidance or insights can be gleaned from these perspectives to help us navigate the potential pitfalls associated with pleasure-seeking?

5. Consider the potential for personal growth and self-discovery that may arise from exploring the dark side of pleasure. How might confronting and understanding the challenges and risks associated with pleasure-seeking lead to greater self-awareness, resilience, and emotional maturity?

(See "8" in the reference section for all references.)

SPIRITUAL DIMENSION OF PLEASURE

The concept of pleasure is a complex and multifaceted phenomenon that can be approached from various perspectives. One of these perspectives is the spiritual dimension of pleasure, which recognizes that pleasure can have a deeper meaning and significance beyond physical gratification. The spiritual dimension emphasizes the role of pleasure in connecting individuals to something greater than themselves and promoting a sense of well-being and fulfillment. Studies have shown that incorporating spirituality into one's life can enhance pleasure and happiness. Park, Koenig, and Park (2015) found that individuals who incorporated spirituality into their daily lives experienced higher levels of life satisfaction, positive emotions, and meaning in life. Similarly, in a qualitative study of individuals who regularly engaged in spiritual practices, Underwood, Teresi, and Gatz (2002) found that participants reported experiencing higher joy, contentment, and overall satisfaction with life. The spiritual dimension of pleasure adds a new and meaningful layer to our understanding of pleasure. It highlights the importance of considering the role of spirituality in our pursuit of happiness and well-being. Incorporating spirituality into our pleasure experiences can deepen and enhance the overall experience, as well as cultivate a more profound sense of purpose and fulfillment. Moreover, the spiritual dimension of pleasure can provide a sense of meaning and purpose in life that is not necessarily derived from physical pleasure alone. This can lead to a deeper understanding of pleasure and a more balanced approach to hedonic pursuits. By incorporating spirituality into our pleasure experiences, we can cultivate a sense of connection to something greater than ourselves, promote a sense of well-being, and deepen our understanding of pleasure as a multifaceted and complex phenomenon. The spiritual dimension of pleasure is an essential aspect to consider when exploring pleasure and well-being. Incorporating spirituality into our pleasure experiences can deepen our understanding of pleasure, promote well-being and fulfillment, and add a meaningful layer to our overall experience of pleasure. By acknowledging the spiritual dimension of pleasure, we can cultivate a more balanced and holistic approach to hedonic pursuits, one that emphasizes the importance of spirituality and connection to something greater than ourselves.

THE ROLE OF PLEASURE IN SPIRITUALITY

The role of pleasure in spirituality is a topic that has been debated for centuries. From a religious perspective, some argue that pleasure can hinder spiritual growth. For instance, in Christianity, the concept of "fornication" is considered a sin, and pleasure derived from sexual behavior is seen as a distraction from spiritual pursuits (1

Corinthians 6:18). Similarly, in Buddhism, the pursuit of sensual pleasure is seen as a source of attachment and suffering, and it is encouraged to focus on spiritual practices that lead to detachment and liberation (The Four Noble Truths). On the other hand, religious perspectives view pleasure as an essential aspect of spiritual growth. For example, in Hinduism, the pursuit of pleasure is seen as a legitimate part of spiritual practice. The idea of "Bhakti," or devotion to a deity, involves experiencing pleasure in one's relationship with the divine (Bhakti Sutras). Similarly, in Sufism, a mystical tradition within Islam, pleasure and joy are essential components of spiritual development and union with the divine (Rumi, "Masnavi"). From a psychological perspective, pleasure can promote spiritual growth by providing a sense of connection and meaning. Research has shown that positive emotions, such as pleasure, can increase connectedness to others and the world (Fredrickson, 2013). This connection can lead to a greater sense of meaning and purpose, an essential aspect of spiritual development (Baumeister & Leary, 1995). Furthermore, pleasure can serve as a motivator for spiritual practice. The pleasure derived from spiritual practices, such as meditation or prayer, can encourage individuals to engage in these practices regularly, leading to a deeper sense of spiritual connection and growth (Ryan & Deci, 2000). The role of pleasure in spirituality is a complex and multidimensional topic that religious leaders and scholars have debated for centuries. While some view pleasure as a hindrance to spiritual growth, others see it as an essential aspect of spiritual development. From a psychological perspective, pleasure can promote spiritual growth by increasing feelings of connection and meaning. Pleasure can also serve as a motivator for spiritual practice. By recognizing the role of pleasure in spirituality, individuals can cultivate a more balanced and holistic approach to spiritual development, one that embraces pleasure as a legitimate aspect of spiritual growth.

THE CONCEPT OF ECSTATIC EXPERIENCES

Ecstatic experiences are intense joy, pleasure, and transcendence beyond everyday human experiences. They are characterized by a sense of detachment from everyday reality and a feeling of being transported to another realm. Various stimuli can trigger ecosystem experiences, including music, dance, spiritual practices, and even drug use. In psychology, ecstatic experiences are often studied as part of the broader concept of altered states of consciousness (ASC). ASC temporarily alters an individual's normal perception, thought, and emotional patterns. Ecstatic experiences are considered a type of ASC because they involve a shift in consciousness that is not part of the individual's everyday experience. Various theories have been developed to explain the underlying mechanisms of ecstatic experiences. For example, some psychologists suggest that these experiences are related to the release of certain neurotransmitters, such as dopamine and serotonin, in the brain. Other researchers have proposed that ecstatic experiences activate specific brain regions, such as the limbic system and the cortex. Ecstatic experiences have also been studied in religious and spiritual communities, where they are often seen as a way to achieve a deeper connection with the divine. In these contexts, ecstatic experiences are often induced through religious or spiritual practices, such as prayer, meditation, or chanting. Ecstatic experiences are intense joy, pleasure, and transcendence beyond everyday human experiences. They are considered a type of altered state of consciousness and have been the subject of study in various fields, including psychology, sociology, and anthropology. Although the underlying mechanisms of these experiences are not yet fully understood, they continue to be an area of active research and investigation.

The concept of ecstatic experiences refers to intense emotional and physical transcendence, often described as overwhelming joy, bliss, or a sense of unity with a greater whole. These experiences are commonly associated with religious or spiritual practices but can also occur in other contexts, such as music, dance, art, or extreme sports (Newberg & Waldman, 2017). Research on ecstatic experiences has shown that they can have significant and long-lasting effects on an individual's well-being, including improvements in mood, creativity, and spirituality (Fink & Benedek, 2014; Maslow, 1964). Furthermore, some studies have suggested that ecstatic experiences can activate the same neural networks as those involved in drug-induced euphoria (Vollenweider & Kometer, 2010), indicating that these experiences may have a powerful impact on the brain. One of the most well-known models of ecstatic experiences is the concept of flow, proposed by psychologist Mihaly Csikszentmihalyi (1990). Flow is described as a state of complete absorption and focus in which an individual is fully immersed in an activity and loses track of time and self-awareness. This state is often associated with joy, creativity, and unity with the task. Another model of ecstatic experiences is the concept of "peak experiences," proposed by humanistic psychologist Abraham Maslow (1964). Peak experiences are moments of intense joy and fulfillment in which an individual feels a sense of unity with the universe and a deep understanding of their place within it. These experiences are often associated with spiritual or mystical experiences but can occur in everyday life. Recent research has also examined the role of brain activity in ecstatic experiences, using techniques such as functional magnetic resonance imaging (fMRI) and electroencephalography (EEG) to measure neural activity during these experiences. Studies have found that these experiences are associated with increased activity in the prefrontal cortex and changes in activity in other brain regions involved in emotion and self-awareness (Newberg & Waldman, 2017). The concept of ecstatic experiences refers to moments of intense emotional and physical transcendence, often associated with religious or spiritual practices, but can also occur in other contexts such as music, dance, art, or extreme sports. These experiences have been shown to have significant and long-lasting effects on an individual's well-being. They may activate the same neural networks as those involved in drug-induced euphoria. Understanding the neural and psychological processes involved in these experiences can have important implications for promoting well-being and personal growth.

THE SEARCH FOR TRANSCENDENCE THROUGH PLEASURE

The pursuit of transcendence through pleasure constitutes an exploration of the idea that individuals endeavor to attain a heightened state of consciousness or a profound connection to a supreme entity by engaging in and appreciating pleasurable experiences. This notion is intrinsically linked to diverse philosophical, religious, and spiritual traditions that underscore the significance of deriving meaning and fulfillment in life through the active pursuit of pleasure. Within this context, pleasure encompasses any experience that evokes a sensation of happiness, gratification, or contentment, manifesting in various forms such as sensory experiences (e.g., gastronomy, auditory stimulation, or artistic expression), physical sensations (e.g., sexual intimacy or physical exertion), and mental or emotional experiences (e.g., affection, mirth, or contemplative practices).

Epicureanism epitomizes a philosophical tradition that accentuates the quest for transcendence through pleasure. Established by the renowned ancient Greek philosopher Epicurus, this school of thought posits that pleasure constitutes the ultimate good, rendering its pursuit the paramount objective of human existence. Epicurus postulated that the trajectory to happiness is contingent upon the circumvention of physical and psychological suffering, as well as the achievement of pleasure through the nurturing of interpersonal relationships, the appreciation of modest pleasures, and the engagement in philosophical discourse.

The quest for transcendence through pleasure, a fundamental aspect of human experience, can be comprehensively explored through the integration of neurobiological, psychological, and spiritual perspectives. At the core of this pursuit lies the brain's intricate reward system, regulated by key neurotransmitters such as dopamine and serotonin. These biochemical messengers are instrumental in modulating pleasurable experiences, which in turn drive behaviors that promote survival and reproduction. Delving deeper into the neurobiological substrates of pleasure-seeking elucidates the complex interplay between these various domains and underscores the multidisciplinary nature of this topic, as well as its significance across a diverse array of scholarly disciplines. <u>From a neurobiological standpoint</u>, the brain's reward system comprises an intricate network of structures, including the ventral tegmental area (VTA), nucleus accumbens (NAc), and the prefrontal cortex (PFC). These regions work in concert to process and evaluate rewarding stimuli, subsequently influencing decision-making, motivation, and goal-directed behaviors. The release of dopamine within this circuitry, particularly from the VTA to the NAc, is associated with the experience of pleasure and reward. Serotonin, on the other hand, plays a more nuanced role in modulating mood, appetite, and social behavior, ultimately shaping the subjective experience of pleasure. <u>In the realm of psychology</u>, the pursuit of pleasure and transcendence is closely linked to concepts such as happiness, well-being, and self-actualization. Positive psychology emphasizes the importance of cultivating positive emotions, engagement, and meaning in life, fostering a deeper understanding of the human capacity for resilience, growth, and flourishing. The quest for transcendence through pleasure can be seen as an integral component of this psychological framework, as individuals continually strive to achieve a heightened sense of fulfillment and personal growth. <u>From a spiritual perspective</u>, the search for transcendence through pleasure may be viewed as an expression of the innate human desire to connect with a higher plane of existence or a more profound sense of self. Throughout history, various religious and spiritual traditions have explored the role of pleasure in facilitating spiritual growth and transformation. For example, the practice of Tantra in Hinduism and Buddhism integrates sensual experiences with meditation and mindfulness, aiming to elevate the practitioner's consciousness to a transcendent state. Similarly, the mystical traditions of Sufism and Kabbalah emphasize the significance of ecstatic experiences, often induced through music, dance, or meditation, in fostering a deeper connection with the divine.

The pursuit of transcendence through pleasure exemplifies the intricate intersection of neurobiology, psychology, and spirituality. By examining the underlying neural mechanisms and their broader implications, researchers can deepen their understanding of the multifaceted nature of pleasure-seeking and its role in human spiritual evolution. This interdisciplinary approach not only reveals the complexity of the human experience but also fosters a more comprehensive and holistic perspective on the pursuit of transcendence and personal growth.

In addition to Epicureanism, other philosophical and spiritual traditions also emphasize the search for transcendence through pleasure. For instance, in the context of Eastern spirituality, Tantra is a practice that seeks to harness the power of pleasure, particularly sexual energy, to attain spiritual enlightenment. Similarly, the Sufi tradition within Islam embraces the concept of transcending the mundane world through ecstatic experiences, often induced by music, dance, or other artistic expressions.

The search for transcendence through pleasure is a complex concept that spans numerous philosophical, religious, and spiritual traditions. It not only delves into the intricacies of human experiences but also reveals the intricate connections between various disciplines. By examining the pursuit of pleasure as a means to attain elevated consciousness or a connection to a higher power, scholars can gain valuable insights into the complexities of human existence, the pursuit of happiness, and the interplay between the physical, emotional, and spiritual aspects of life.

Another example is the Hindu philosophy of Tantra, which emphasizes the use of pleasure as a means of achieving spiritual transcendence. When approached with mindfulness and intention, Tantra teaches that pleasure can be used to awaken the individual's consciousness and connect them with the divine. Through practices such as meditation, ritual, and sexual union, individuals are said to be able to experience a state of pure consciousness and transcend the limitations of the physical world. It is important to note that the search for transcendence through pleasure is not limited to specific philosophical or religious traditions. Many individuals, regardless of their cultural or spiritual background, may experience a sense of connection to something more significant through the pursuit and enjoyment of pleasure.

<u>Reflective Questions:</u>

1. How do various spiritual traditions and practices address the concept of pleasure? Are there specific teachings or beliefs about pleasure within your own spiritual or philosophical framework that resonate with or challenge your understanding of the role of pleasure in your life?

2. In what ways can the pursuit of pleasure be integrated with spiritual growth and development? Can you identify any specific spiritual practices or experiences that have led to a deeper understanding or appreciation of pleasure in your life?

3. Reflect on the potential connection between pleasure and transcendent experiences, such as feelings of awe, wonder, or unity with a higher power. How might these experiences provide insight into the spiritual dimensions of pleasure and contribute to our overall well-being?

4. How do spiritual traditions address the potential pitfalls or dangers associated with the pursuit of pleasure, such as hedonism, addiction, or attachment? What guidance or practices might these traditions offer to help us cultivate a balanced and mindful approach to seeking pleasure?

5. In what ways can engaging with the spiritual dimension of pleasure inspire a deeper sense of meaning, purpose, and fulfillment in our lives? How might a greater understanding of the spiritual aspects of pleasure inform our choices and priorities in the pursuit of happiness and well-being?

(See number "9" in the reference section for all references)

ART OF PLEASURE

The art of pleasure embodies the conscious and purposeful cultivation of experiences that evoke joy, happiness, and satisfaction within one's existence. This notion encompasses a wide array of activities, ranging from the simple gratifications of relishing a delectable meal or immersing oneself in the natural world, to more intricate experiences such as engaging in artistic expression or delving into sensual intimacy. The pursuit of pleasure is frequently perceived as a means to enhance one's life and imbue it with meaning, serving as a central motif in myriad philosophical, spiritual, and cultural traditions across the annals of history.In recent years, the concept of the art of pleasure has witnessed a surge in attention and popularity, with a growing number of individuals striving to prioritize pleasure in their lives and designate it as a focal point of their personal development and self-exploration. This burgeoning interest has given rise to an expanding corpus of research and literature on the subject, examining the ways in which pleasure can be nurtured and assimilated into everyday life. Within the context of philosophy and psychology, the art of pleasure can be linked to theories such as hedonism, which posits that pleasure is the primary intrinsic good and ultimate aim of human existence. In this light, the deliberate cultivation of pleasurable experiences can be seen as a rational and valuable endeavor in the pursuit of a meaningful and fulfilling life. Moreover, the art of pleasure intersects with the concept of well-being, which encompasses subjective happiness, life satisfaction, and the presence of positive emotions. From the perspective of positive psychology, the conscious pursuit of pleasure may contribute to increased well-being by fostering a sense of contentment, resilience, and personal fulfillment. Culturally, the art of pleasure can be seen as a reflection of shifting societal values and attitudes. In contemporary society, where material wealth and success are often prioritized, the renewed focus on pleasure as a vital component of a meaningful life challenges traditional norms and invites individuals to reevaluate their priorities and aspirations. The art of pleasure also bears relevance to the study of human relationships and interpersonal dynamics. As individuals consciously engage in the pursuit of pleasurable experiences, they may simultaneously deepen their connections with others and foster a greater sense of empathy, understanding, and emotional intimacy. Furthermore, the exploration of the art of pleasure may offer valuable insights into the potential therapeutic applications of pleasurable experiences. By understanding the neurobiological and psychological mechanisms underpinning pleasure, researchers and clinicians may develop novel interventions and treatment strategies aimed at enhancing well-being and ameliorating psychological distress. The art of pleasure constitutes a multifaceted and evolving concept that transcends disciplines and permeates various aspects of human life. As individuals and society increasingly prioritize and integrate pleasure into their lives, they stand to reap the benefits of enriched experiences, deeper connections, and a heightened sense of meaning and fulfillment. By examining the art of pleasure through the lenses of philosophy, psychology, culture, and interpersonal dynamics, we can further our understanding of this intriguing phenomenon and its implications for human flourishing.

THE ROLE OF ART IN PLEASURE

Art has served as a wellspring of pleasure for humanity since its earliest manifestations. From the rudimentary cave paintings to the most resplendent works of architecture and literature, art possesses the capacity to elate, inspire, and elevate the human spirit. The function of art in the realm of pleasure is intricate and multifaceted, spanning an array of sensory, emotional, intellectual, and spiritual experiences. One of the primary means by which art contributes to pleasure lies in its ability to stimulate the senses. Visual art forms, such as painting, sculpture, and photography, have the potential to generate captivating and thought-provoking aesthetic experiences. Similarly, music, dance, and theater engage the senses and facilitate visceral encounters with emotions and ideas. Beyond the sensory realm, art serves as a conduit for intellectual pleasure, provoking introspection and contemplation of concepts that extend beyond our immediate reality. Furthermore, art contributes to pleasure by providing a platform for expression and connection. It can forge bonds among individuals, generating shared experiences that cultivate empathy, understanding, and camaraderie. Art also functions as a vehicle for personal expression, empowering individuals to explore and articulate their most profound thoughts and emotions in a creative and meaningful manner. Art's capacity to offer escape and transcendence constitutes another facet of its role in pleasure. It can transport us to alternate realms and eras, enabling us to surmount the confines of our existence. Art can also evoke a sense of beauty, awe, and wonder that extracts us from the mundanity of daily life, imbuing our experiences with joy and enchantment. Moreover, the study of art's relationship with pleasure extends to various academic disciplines, such as aesthetics, sociology, and psychology. Aesthetics explores the nature of beauty, taste, and the appreciation of art, while sociological and psychological perspectives examine the impact of art on individual and collective well-being, as well as its capacity to foster social cohesion and promote emotional and cognitive growth. The interplay between art and pleasure is not only multifaceted and complex but also dynamic, as it evolves alongside cultural and technological advancements. In the digital age, the proliferation of new media and artistic forms further expands the scope of sensory, emotional, intellectual, and spiritual experiences available to individuals, potentially redefining the boundaries of pleasure in art. The role of art in pleasure encompasses a diverse range of experiences, transcending the sensory and extending into the emotional, intellectual, and spiritual domains. Whether marveling at a mesmerizing painting, immersing oneself in an evocative musical composition, or delving into an exceptional work of literature, art possesses the power to inspire, gratify, and elevate us in innumerable ways. By examining the multifaceted nature of art's relationship with pleasure, we can deepen our understanding of this fascinating interplay and its implications for the human experience.

THE AESTHETICS OF PLEASURE

The aesthetics of pleasure is a philosophical concept that deals with the nature and qualities of pleasure experienced through art and other aesthetic objects. It is an important area of study in aesthetics, the branch of philosophy that deals with the nature of art, beauty, and taste. One of the central questions in the aesthetics of pleasure is what makes an object aesthetically pleasurable. There are different theories and approaches to answering this question, and some of them are discussed below.

1. Formalism: This theory holds that the aesthetic pleasure derived from an object results from its formal qualities, such as symmetry, balance, and harmony. According to formalists, the beauty of an object is independent of its content or meaning and is purely a matter of its formal properties. This view is associated with the philosopher Immanuel Kant, who argued that aesthetic pleasure is derived from how an object is organized and presented to the senses.

2. Emotionalism: This theory posits that aesthetic pleasure arises from the emotional response that an object evokes in the viewer or audience. This view is associated with the philosopher Arthur Schopenhauer, who believed that aesthetic pleasure is a result of the object's ability to arouse emotions and engage the viewer's imagination. Emotionalists argue that art is successful when it elicits a strong emotional response, whether it is joy, sadness, fear, or awe.

3. Expressionism: This theory emphasizes the expressive qualities of art and holds that aesthetic pleasure results from the object's ability to express human emotions, ideas, or values. Expressionists argue that art succeeds when it communicates something about the human condition or the artist's experience. This view is associated with the philosopher Friedrich Nietzsche, who believed that art is a form of self-expression that reveals the artist's most

profound thoughts and feelings.

4. <u>Cognitive Theories</u>: This theory holds that aesthetic pleasure arises from an object's intellectual engagement with the viewer or audience. Cognitive theorists argue that art is successful when it challenges the viewer's beliefs, assumptions, and expectations and forces them to reevaluate their understanding of the world. This view is associated with the philosopher John Dewey, who believed that an aesthetic experience is a form of inquiry that leads to a deeper understanding of oneself and the world.

The aesthetics of pleasure is a complex and multifaceted concept explored by many philosophers throughout history. It is worth noting that these theories are not mutually exclusive, and some artworks can evoke pleasure through a combination of these approaches. For example, a painting may be aesthetically pleasing because of its formal qualities such as color, texture, and composition, but it may also evoke emotions or express ideas about the human condition. The different theories of aesthetic pleasure offer different insights into what makes an object aesthetically pleasing. It is up to the viewer or audience to determine which theory resonates with their experiences of aesthetic pleasure.

THE ART OF CREATING PLEASURE

The art of creating pleasure refers to the ability to design experiences that evoke positive emotions and sensations in people. This can be achieved through various means, such as aesthetics, functionality, sensory stimulation, or emotional connection. It is a critical aspect of design, marketing, and customer experience management, as it can influence people's behavior, perception, and loyalty toward products or services. To create pleasure, designers and marketers need to deeply understand the target audience's needs, preferences, and values. They also need to consider the context, setting, and situation in which the experience will occur. For example, a restaurant that serves gourmet food may create pleasure through its sophisticated ambiance, attentive service, and exquisite presentation of dishes. Another example of the art of creating pleasure is in product design. Products that are aesthetically pleasing, ergonomic, and user-friendly can make a positive emotional response in users, leading to increased satisfaction and loyalty. Apple Inc. is a prime example of a company that has mastered the art of creating pleasure through its product design, which has helped the company become one of the most valuable in the world.

Furthermore, sensory stimulation can also create pleasure. For instance, music, colors, textures, and scents can all evoke positive emotions and enhance the overall experience. This is particularly relevant in the hospitality industry, where hotels and resorts often use sensory elements to create a unique and memorable experience for their guests. Creating pleasure is about designing experiences that evoke positive emotions and sensations in people. It requires an understanding of the audience's needs, preferences, and values and the ability to create an experience that satisfies them. By mastering this art, designers and marketers can create a solid emotional connection with their audience, increasing customer satisfaction, loyalty, and revenue.

One related idea is the concept of user-centered design. User-centered design is a design approach that prioritizes the needs and preferences of the user when designing products or services. This approach involves understanding the target audience's goals, behaviors, and challenges to create designs that meet their needs and expectations. User-centered design is essential for creating pleasure in products or services as it ensures that the design is tailored to the user's preferences, making the experience more enjoyable and satisfying.

An additional concept intimately connected to the relationship between art and pleasure is the notion of emotional design. Emotional design encompasses the utilization of design elements to evoke emotional reactions in individuals. By eliciting positive emotions such as joy, excitement, or nostalgia, emotional design can engender pleasure in users. This approach entails crafting products or services that are not only functionally effective but also aesthetically appealing and emotionally resonant. Emotional design can be actualized through a diverse array of techniques, including the manipulation of color, form, texture, and sound. By fostering emotional connections with users, emotional design can enhance engagement, foster loyalty, and amplify satisfaction. The concept of emotional design transcends mere visual appeal, as it delves into the psychological and emotional dimensions of human experience, addressing the more profound and nuanced aspects of human-product inte ractions.The theoretical underpinnings of emotional design can be traced to the work of cognitive scientist and usability expert Donald Norman. Norman posited that the design of products and services should cater to three distinct levels of human cognition: visceral, behavioral, and reflective. The visceral level pertains to the immediate, instinctual reactions to sensory stimuli; the behavioral level relates to the user's experience in terms of functionality and usability; and the reflective level encompasses the user's conscious thoughts and feelings about the product or service. By addressing each of these levels, emotional design aims to create harmonious and gratifying experiences for users. Emotional design can also be viewed through the lens of neuroaesthetics, an interdisciplinary field that explores the neural basis of aesthetic experiences. Research in neuroaesthetics has demonstrated that the brain's reward system, mediated by neurotransmitters such as dopamine and serotonin, plays a critical role in our appreciation of beauty and emotionally evocative design. This neurological perspective highlights the interplay between design, emotion, and cognitive processes, further supporting the significance of emotional design in fostering pleasure. Moreover, the implications of emotional design extend beyond individual experiences to encompass broader societal and economic ramifications. In an increasingly competitive marketplace, emotionally resonant design can serve as a differentiating factor for businesses, enhancing brand recognition and customer retention. Furthermore, emotional design can contribute to the overall well-being of users by generating positive emotional experiences that complement the functional aspects of products and services. In the context of the digital age, emotional design takes on new dimensions as it adapts to the rapidly evolving landscape of technology and user interfaces. The incorporation of emotional design principles in virtual environments, artificial intelligence, and other emerging technologies can lead to more intuitive, engaging, and emotionally satisfying experiences for users. Emotional design represents a multifaceted and dynamic concept that seeks to evoke emotional responses and generate pleasure through the thoughtful integration of design elements. By addressing the visceral, behavioral, and reflective levels of human cognition, emotional design aims to create products and services that are not only functionally effective but also aesthetically and emotionally satisfying. The exploration of emotional design, its neurological underpinnings, and its broader implications for society and the economy provides valuable insights into the complex interplay between design, emotion, and human experience.

Reflective questions for readers:

1. How have your experiences with various forms of art, such as visual art, music, dance, or literature, contributed to your understanding and appreciation of pleasure? Can you identify specific artistic experiences that have evoked a strong sense of pleasure or emotional resonance?

2. Reflect on the ways in which the art of pleasure can be cultivated and nurtured in your daily life. Are there specific activities, practices, or experiences that you might consider integrating into your routine to enhance your connection with the art of pleasure?

3. In what ways can the art of pleasure be used as a tool for personal growth, self-discovery, and emotional healing? How might engaging with artistic expressions of pleasure provide insights into your own emotions, desires, and

experiences?

4. How do societal and cultural factors influence our understanding of the art of pleasure and our ability to engage with it fully? Are there specific cultural or societal barriers that might limit our access to or appreciation of the art of pleasure, and how might we overcome these obstacles?

5. Consider the potential benefits of embracing the art of pleasure in the context of building and maintaining relationships, both with ourselves and with others. How might cultivating a deeper connection with the art of pleasure enhance our capacity for empathy, understanding, and emotional connection in our interactions with others?

(See "10" in the reference section for all references.)

<u>REFERENCES</u>

0.1
Berridge, K. C. (2003). Pleasures of the brain. Brain and Cognition, 52(1), 106-128. doi: 10.1016/S0278-2626(03)00014-9
Diener, E., Lucas, R. E., & Oishi, S. (2017). Advances and open questions in the science of subjective well-being. Collabra: Psychology, 3(1), 6. doi: 10.1525/collabra.85
Hansen, T., Elliott, M. T., & Griego, O. V. (2015). Pleasure and productivity: The happy link. Journal of Happiness Studies, 16(3), 557-571. doi: 10.1007/s10902-014-9518-6
Kashdan, T. B., Biswas-Diener, R., & King, L. A. (2008). Reconsidering happiness: The costs of distinguishing between hedonics and eudaimonia. The Journal of Positive Psychology, 3(4), 219-233. doi: 10.1080/17439760802303044
Twenge, J. M., Cooper, A. B., Joiner, T. E., Duffy, M. E., & Binau, S. G. (2020). Age, period, and cohort trends in mood disorder indicators and suicide-related outcomes in a nationally representative dataset, 2005-2017. Journal of Abnormal Psychology, 129(5), 526-536. doi: 10.1037/abn0000510

1
Kringelbach, M. L. (2019). The pleasure center: Trust your animal instincts. Scientific American.
Panksepp, J. (2011). The basic emotional circuits of mammalian brains: Do animals have affective lives?. Neuroscience and biobehavioral reviews, 35(9), 1791-1804.
Ryan, R. M., & Deci, E. L. (2001). On happiness and human potentials: A review of research on hedonic and eudaimonic well-being. Annual review of psychology, 52(1), 141-166.

1.1
Berridge, K. C., & Kringelbach, M. L. (2015). Pleasure systems in the brain. Neuron, 86(3), 646-664. https://doi.org/10.1016/j.neuron.2015.02.018
Kringelbach, M. L. (2005). The human orbitofrontal cortex: linking reward to hedonic experience. Nature Reviews Neuroscience, 6(9), 691-702. https://doi.org/10.1038/nrn1747
Mikulincer, M., & Shaver, P. R. (2016). Attachment in adulthood: Structure, dynamics, and change. Guilford Publications.
Zagon, I. S., & McLaughlin, P. J. (2014). Endogenous opioids and the therapeutic use of low-dose naltrexone for opioid and alcohol dependence. American Journal of Drug and Alcohol Abuse, 40(6), 369-378. https://doi.org/10.3109/00952990.2014.933840

2
Kringelbach, M. L., & Berridge, K. C. (2012). The Joyful Mind. Scientific American, 306(2), 56-63. https://doi.org/10.1038/scientificamerican0212-56
Panksepp, J. (1998). Affective neuroscience: The foundations of human and animal emotions. Oxford University Press.
Robinson, T. E., & Berridge, K. C. (2003). Addiction. Annual Review of Psychology, 54(1), 25-53. https://doi.org/10.1146/annurev.psych.54.101601.145237
Scherer, K. R. (2005). What are emotions? And how can they be measured? Social Science Information, 44(4), 695-729. https://doi.org/10.1177/0539018405058216

2.1
Kringelbach, M. L., & Berridge, K. C. (2010). The functional neuroanatomy of pleasure and happiness. In D. Y. Kim (Ed.), Handbook of behavior genetics (pp. 305-325). Springer.
Berridge, K. C., & Kringelbach, M. L. (2015). Pleasure systems in the brain. Neuron, 86(3), 646-664. https://doi.org/10.1016/j.neuron.2015.02.018
Fishbein, M., & Ajzen, I. (2010). Predicting and changing behavior: The reasoned action approach. Psychology Press.
Knobloch-Westerwick, S., & Meng, J. (2009). Looking the other way: Selective exposure to attitude-consistent and counter-attitudinal political information. Communication Research, 36(3), 426-448. https://doi.org/10.1177/0093650209332392

Fredrickson, B. L., & Losada, M. F. (2005). Positive affect and the complex dynamics of human flourishing. American Psychologist, 60(7), 678-686. https://doi.org/10.1037/0003-066X.60.7.678

Pressman, S. D., Cohen, S., Miller, G. E., Barkin, A., Rabin, B. S., & Treanor, J. J. (2005). Loneliness, social network size, and immune response to influenza vaccination in college freshmen. Health Psychology, 24(3), 297-306. https://doi.org/10.1037/0278-6133.24.3.297

2.2

Duhigg, C. (2012). The power of habit: Why we do what we do in life and business. Random House.

Fredrickson, B. L. (2001). The role of positive emotions in positive psychology: The broaden-and-build theory of positive emotions. American psychologist, 56(3), 218.

Gable, S. L., Reis, H. T., Impett, E. A., & Asher, E. R. (2004). What do you do when things go right? The intrapersonal and interpersonal benefits of sharing positive events. Journal of personality and social psychology, 87(2), 228.

Patrick, H., Williams, G. C., & Niemiec, C. P. (2013). The health care professional as personal coach: Increasing healthy lifestyle behaviors through the application of motivational interviewing. American journal of lifestyle medicine, 7(1), 31-38.

Pressman, S. D., & Cohen, S. (2005). Does positive affect influence health?. Psychological bulletin, 131(6), 925.

Riggio, R. E., & Throckmorton, B. (2001). The social context of emotional experiences: A research agenda for the 21st century. Journal of Social and Clinical Psychology, 20(1), 3-12.

Ryan, R. M., & Deci, E. L. (2001). On happiness and human potentials: A review of research on hedonic and eudaimonic well-being. Annual review of psychology, 52(1), 141-166.

2.3

Chida, Y., & Steptoe, A. (2008). Positive psychological well-being and mortality: a quantitative review of prospective observational studies. Psychosomatic Medicine, 70(7), 741-756.

Garland, E. L., Farb, N. A., Goldin, P. R., & Fredrickson, B. L. (2015). Mindfulness broadens awareness and builds eudaimonic meaning: A process model of mindful positive emotion regulation. Psychological Inquiry, 26(4), 293-314.

Kringelbach, M. L., & Berridge, K. C. (2010). The neuroscience of happiness and pleasure. Social Research: An International Quarterly, 77(2), 659-678.

Nussbaum, M. C. (1990). Love's knowledge: Books on philosophy and literature. Oxford University Press.

Pressman, S. D., & Cohen, S. (2005). Does positive affect influence health? Psychological Bulletin, 131(6), 925-971.

Wolf, S. (2010). Meaning in life and why it matters. Princeton University Press.

2.4

Berridge, K. C., & Kringelbach, M. L. (2015). Pleasure systems in the brain. Neuron, 86(3), 646-664.

Kringelbach, M. L., & Berridge, K. C. (2010). Pleasures of the brain. Oxford University Press.

Panksepp, J., & Biven, L. (2012). The archaeology of mind: Neuroevolutionary origins of human emotions. WW Norton & Company.

2.5

Berridge, K. C. (2007). The debate over dopamine's role in reward: The case for incentive salience. Psychopharmacology, 191(3), 391-431.

Gill, R., & Orgad, S. (2017). The amazing bounce-backable woman: Resilience and the psychological turn in neoliberalism. Feminist Media Studies, 17(4), 609-625.

Haybron, D. M. (2008). Philosophy and the science of subjective well-being. In M. Eid & R. J. Larsen (Eds.), The science of subjective well-being (pp. 17-43). Guilford Press.

2.6

Berridge, K. C. (2009). 'Wanting' and 'liking': Observations from the neuroscience and psychology laboratory. Inquiry, 52(4), 378-398.

Fava, G. A., & Tomba, E. (2010). Increasing psychological well-being and resilience by psychotherapeutic methods. Journal of Personality, 78(6), 1475-1506.

Koob, G. F., & Volkow, N. D. (2016). Neurobiology of addiction: a neurocircuitry analysis. The Lancet Psychiatry, 3(8), 760-773.

Nestler, E. J., & Carlezon, W. A. (2006). The mesolimbic dopamine reward circuit in depression. Biological psychiatry, 59(12), 1151-1159.

Volkow, N. D., Wang, G. J., Fowler, J. S., Tomasi, D., & Telang, F. (2010). Addiction: beyond dopamine reward circuitry. Proceedings of the National Academy of Sciences, 107(10), 8877-8882.

3

Berridge, K. C., & Kringelbach, M. L. (2015). Pleasure systems in the brain. Neuron, 86(3), 646-664.

Koob, G. F., & Volkow, N. D. (2016). Neurobiology of addiction: a neurocircuitry analysis. The Lancet Psychiatry, 3(8), 760-773.

Salamone, J. D., Correa, M., Farrar, A. M., Nunes, E. J., & Pardo, M. (2009). Dopamine, behavioral economics, and effort. Frontiers in behavioral neuroscience, 3, 13.

3.1

Berridge, K. C., & Kringelbach, M. L. (2015). Pleasure systems in the brain. Neuron, 86(3), 646-664. https://doi.org/10.1016/j.neuron.2015.02.018

Kringelbach, M. L., & Berridge, K. C. (2009). Towards a functional neuroanatomy of pleasure and happiness. Trends in cognitive sciences, 13(11), 479-487. https://doi.org/10.1016/j.tics.2009.08.006

Lindquist, K. A., Wager, T. D., Kober, H., Bliss-Moreau, E., & Barrett, L. F. (2012). The brain basis of emotion: A meta-analytic review. Behavioral and Brain Sciences, 35(3), 121-143. https://doi.org/10.1017/S0140525X11000446

Knutson, B., & Cooper, J. C. (2005). Functional magnetic resonance imaging of reward prediction. Current opinion in neurology, 18(4), 411-417. https://doi.org/10.1097/01.wco.0000173463.24780.37

O'Doherty, J., Dayan, P., Schultz, J., Deichmann, R., Friston, K., & Dolan, R. J. (2004). Dissociable roles of ventral and dorsal striatum in instrumental conditioning. Science, 304(5669), 452-454. https://doi.org/10.1126/science.1094285

Kringelbach, M. L., & Berridge, K. C. (2009). Towards a functional neuroanatomy of pleasure and happiness. Trends in cognitive sciences, 13(11), 479-487. https://doi.org/10.1016/j.tics.2009.08.006

Rolls, E. T. (2019). Brain mechanisms of pleasure and liking. Philosophical Transactions of the Royal Society B, 374(1785), 20190367. https://doi.org/10.1098/rstb.2019.0367

Salimpoor, V. N., van den Bosch, I., Kovacevic, N., McIntosh, A. R., Dagher, A., & Zatorre, R. J. (2013). Interactions between the nucleus accumbens and auditory cortices predict music reward value. Science, 340(6129), 216-219. https://doi.org/10.1126/science.1231059

Hebb, D. O. (1955). Drives and the CNS (conceptual nervous system). Psychological Review, 62(4), 243-254. https://doi.org/10.1037/h0041825

Kringelbach, M. L., & Berridge, K. C. (2010). The functional neuroanatomy of pleasure and happiness. Discovery Medicine, 9(49), 579-587. https://pubmed.ncbi.nlm.nih.gov/20587367/

Leknes, S., & Tracey, I. (2008). A common neurobiology for pain and pleasure. Nature Reviews Neuroscience, 9(4), 314-320. https://doi.org/10.1038/nrn2333

Salimpoor, V. N., Benovoy, M., Larcher, K., Dagher, A., & Zatorre, R. J. (2011). Anatomically distinct dopamine release during anticipation and experience of peak emotion to music. Nature Neuroscience, 14(2), 257-262. https://doi.org/10.1038/nn.2726

Schultz, W. (2000). Multiple reward signals in the brain. Nature Reviews Neuroscience, 1(3), 199-207. https://doi.org/10.1038/35044563

Wise, R. A. (2002). Brain reward circuitry: insights from unsensed incentives. Neuron, 36(2), 229-240. https://doi.org/10.1016/S0896-6273(02)00965-0

3.12

Bogdan, R., Baranger, D. A. A., & Agrawal, A. (2016). Polygenic risk scores in clinical psychology: Bridging genomic risk to individual differences. Annual Review of Clinical Psychology, 12, 335-362.

Gard, D. E., Kring, A. M., Gard, M. G., Horan, W. P., & Green, M. F. (2007). Anhedonia in schizophrenia: Distinctions between anticipatory and consummatory pleasure. Schizophrenia Research, 93(1-3), 253-260.

Mason, L., O'Sullivan, N., Blackburn, M., Bentall, R., & El-Deredy, W. (2012). I want it now! Neural correlates of hypersensitivity to immediate reward in hypomania. Biological Psychiatry, 71(6), 530-537.

Pizzagalli, D. A. (2014). Depression, stress, and anhedonia: Toward a synthesis and integrated model. Annual Review of Clinical Psychology, 10, 393-423.

Rizvi, S. J., Pizzagalli, D. A., Sproule, B. A., & Kennedy, S. H. (2016). Assessing anhedonia in depression: Potentials and pitfalls. Neuroscience and Biobehavioral Reviews, 65, 21-35.

Treadway, M. T., & Zald, D. H. (2011). Reconsidering anhedonia in depression: Lessons from translational neuroscience. Neuroscience and Biobehavioral Reviews, 35(3), 537-555.

Volkow, N. D., & Morales, M. (2015). The brain on drugs: From reward to addiction. Cell, 162(4), 712-725.

Whitton, A. E., Treadway, M. T., & Pizzagalli, D. A. (2015). Reward processing dysfunction in major depression, bipolar disorder and schizophrenia. Current Opinion in Psychiatry, 28(1), 7-12.

3.2

Bechara, A. (2005). Decision making, impulse control and loss of willpower to resist drugs: A neurocognitive perspective. Nature Neuroscience, 8(11), 1458-1463.

Bickel, W. K., Koffarnus, M. N., Moody, L., & Wilson, A. G. (2014). The behavioral- and neuro-economic process of temporal discounting: A candidate behavioral marker of addiction. Neuropharmacology, 76, 518-527.

Kringelbach, M. L., de Araujo, I. E., & Rolls, E. T. (2012). Taste-related activity in the human dorsolateral prefrontal cortex. Neuroimage, 61(3), 781-788.

Rolls, E. T. (2016). Limbic systems for emotion and for memory, but no single limbic system. Cortex, 74, 17-38.

Bartra, O., McGuire, J. T., & Kable, J. W. (2013). The valuation system: a coordinate-based meta-analysis of BOLD fMRI experiments examining neural correlates of subjective value. NeuroImage, 76, 412-427. doi: 10.1016/j.neuroimage.2013.02.063

Kringelbach, M. L., & Berridge, K. C. (2009). Towards a functional neuroanatomy of pleasure and happiness. Trends in Cognitive Sciences, 13(11), 479-487. doi: 10.1016/j.tics.2009.08.006

Schultz, W. (2015). Neuronal reward and decision signals: from theories to data. Physiological Reviews, 95(3), 853-951. doi: 10.1152/physrev.00023.2014

3.3

LeDoux, J. (2000). Emotion circuits in the brain. Annual Review of Neuroscience, 23, 155-184.

Squire, L. R. (1992). Memory and the hippocampus: A synthesis from findings with rats, monkeys, and humans. Psychological Review, 99(2), 195-231.

Swanson, L. W. (2000). What is the limbic system? Neuroscience & Biobehavioral Reviews, 24(5), 591-611.

3.4

Berridge, K. C., & Kringelbach, M. L. (2015). Pleasure systems in the brain. Neuron, 86(3), 646-664.

Davidson, R. J., & Irwin, W. (1999). The functional neuroanatomy of emotion and affective style. Trends in cognitive sciences, 3(1), 11-21.

Phelps, E. A. (2004). Human emotion and memory: interactions of the amygdala and hippocampal complex. Current opinion in neurobiology, 14(2), 198-202.

Rolls, E. T. (2005). Taste, olfactory, and food texture processing in the brain, and the control of food intake. Physiology & behavior, 85(1), 45-56.

Schultz, W. (2015). Neuronal reward and decision signals: from theories to data. Physiological reviews, 95(3), 853-951.

Wise, R. A. (2004). Dopamine, learning and motivation. Nature reviews neuroscience, 5(6), 483-494.

3.5

Berridge, K. C., & Kringelbach, M. L. (2013). Neuroscience of affect: brain mechanisms of pleasure and displeasure. Current Opinion in Neurobiology, 23(3), 294-303.

Everitt, B. J., & Robbins, T. W. (2016). Drug addiction: updating actions to habits to compulsions ten years on. Annual Review of Psychology, 67, 23-50.

Frank, M. J., Seeberger, L. C., & O'Reilly, R. C. (2004). By carrot or by stick: cognitive reinforcement learning in parkinsonism. Science, 306(5703), 1940-1943.

Nestler, E. J., & Carlezon Jr, W. A. (2006). The mesolimbic dopamine reward circuit in depression. Biological Psychiatry, 59(12), 1151-1159.

Schultz, W. (2006). Behavioral theories and the neurophysiology of reward. Annual Review of Psychology, 57, 87-115.

3.6

Garland, E. L., Froeliger, B., & Howard, M. O. (2014). Mindfulness training targets neurocognitive mechanisms of addiction at the attention-appraisal-emotion interface. Frontiers in Psychiatry, 4, 173.

Goldin, P. R., & Gross, J. J. (2010). Effects of mindfulness-based stress reduction (MBSR) on emotion regulation in social anxiety disorder. Emotion, 10(1), 83–91.

Kringelbach, M. L., & Berridge, K. C. (2010). Pleasures of the Brain. Oxford University Press.

Smoski, M. J., Felder, J., Bizzell, J., Green, S. R., Ernst, M., Lynch, T. R., & Dichter, G. S. (2014). fMRI of alterations in reward selection, anticipation, and feedback in major depressive disorder. Journal of Affective

Disorders, 152-154, 63-73.

Volkow, N. D., & Morales, M. (2015). The brain on drugs: From reward to addiction. Cell, 162(4), 712–725.

Dreher, J. C., & Schmidt, P. J. (2008). Dopamine and decision-making in addiction: a review of the literature. In Progress in brain research (Vol. 172, pp. 193-214). Elsevier.

Howes, O. D., & Kapur, S. (2014). The dopamine hypothesis of schizophrenia: version III--the final common pathway. Schizophrenia bulletin, 40(3), 537-545.

Paulus, M. P., & Stein, M. B. (2006). An insular view of anxiety. Biological psychiatry, 60(4), 383-387.

Snaith, R. P., Bridge, G. W., & Hamilton, M. (1995). The depressive experience in primary care: symptomatology and sub-syndromal mood disorders. International Journal of Psychiatry in Clinical Practice, 1(sup1), S3-S7.

Volkow, N. D., Koob, G. F., & McLellan, A. T. (2016). Neurobiologic advances from the brain disease model of addiction. New England Journal of Medicine, 374(4), 363-371.

Volkow, N. D., Wang, G. J., & Baler, R. D. (2013). Reward, dopamine and the control of food intake: implications for obesity. Trends in cognitive sciences, 17(5), 293-302.

Frank, G. K., Shott, M. E., Hagman, J. O., & Mittal, V. A. (2012). Alterations in brain structures related to taste reward circuitry in ill and recovered anorexia nervosa and in bulimia nervosa. American Journal of Psychiatry, 169(10), 1153-1161.

Gola, M., Wordecha, M., Sescousse, G., Lew-Starowicz, M., Kossowski, B., Wypych, M., ... & Marchewka, A. (2017). Can pornography be addictive? An fMRI study of men seeking treatment for problematic pornography use. Neuropsychopharmacology, 42(10), 2021-2031.

Koob, G. F., & Volkow, N. D. (2016). Neurobiology of addiction: a neurocircuitry analysis. The Lancet Psychiatry, 3(8), 760-773.

Nestler, E. J., & Carlezon Jr, W. A. (2006). The mesolimbic dopamine reward circuit in depression. Biological psychiatry, 59(12), 1151-1159.

Potenza, M. N. (2008). The neurobiology of pathological gambling and drug addiction: an overview and new findings. Philosophical Transactions of the Royal Society B: Biological Sciences, 363(1507), 3181-3189.

Kühn, S., & Gallinat, J. (2016). Neurobiological basis of hypersexuality. International review of neurobiology, 129, 67-83.

Kuss, D. J., & Griffiths, M. D. (2012). Internet gaming addiction: A systematic review of empirical research. International journal of mental health and addiction, 10(2), 278-296.

Linnet, J., Peterson, E., Doudet, D. J., Gjedde, A., & Møller, A. (2011). Dopamine release in ventral striatum during Iowa Gambling Task performance is associated with increased excitement levels in pathological gambling. Addiction, 106(2), 383-390.

Smith, M. A., Lynch, W. J., & Exercise, A. S. A. P. (2015). Exercise as a potential treatment for drug abuse: evidence from preclinical studies. Frontiers in psychiatry, 6, 88.

Voon, V., Derbyshire, K., Rück, C., Irvine, M. A., Worbe, Y., Enander, J., ... & Robbins, T. W. (2015). Disorders of compulsivity: a common bias towards learning habits. Molecular psychiatry, 20(3), 345-352.

Becker, S. J., Spirito, A., Hernandez, L., Barnett, N. P., Eaton, C. A., Lewander, W., & Marcella, J. (2016). Trajectories of adolescent alcohol use after brief treatment in an emergency department. Drug and Alcohol Dependence, 163, S17-S22.

Garland, E. L., Froeliger, B., & Howard, M. O. (2015). Mindfulness training targets neurocognitive mechanisms of addiction at the attention-appraisal-emotion interface. Frontiers in Psychiatry, 6, 173.

Hawton, K., & van Heeringen, K. (Eds.). (2009). The international handbook of suicide prevention: Research, policy and practice. John Wiley & Sons.

Katz, D. A., McHale, J. P., & D'Angelo, H. (2019). Stress reduction and mindfulness techniques in addiction recovery. Journal of Mental Health Counseling, 41(2), 100-114.

Kelly, J. F., Pagano, M. E., Stout, R. L., Johnson, S. M., & Delaney, H. D. (2012). The role of Alcoholics Anonymous in mobilizing adaptive social network changes: A prospective lagged mediational analysis. Drug and Alcohol Dependence, 121(3), 213-218.

NIDA. (2020). Preventing Drug Use among Children and Adolescents (In Brief). National Institute on Drug Abuse. https://www.drugabuse.gov/publications/preventing-drug-use-among-children-adolescents-in-brief

SAMHSA. (2014). The Role of Behavioral Health in Preventing Prescription Opioid Overdose. Substance Abuse and Mental Health Services Administration. https://store.samhsa.gov/product/The-Role-of-Behavioral-Health-in-Preventing-Prescription-Opioid-Overdose/SMA14-4742

National Council for Behavioral Health. (2020). Suicide Prevention. https://www.thenationalcouncil.org/topics/suicide-prevention/

Substance Abuse and Mental Health Services Administration. (2020). Prevention of Substance Abuse and Mental Illness. https://www.samhsa.gov/prevention

American Psychiatric Association. (2017). Practice Guideline for the Pharmacological Treatment of Patients With Alcohol Use Disorder. American Psychiatric Association Publishing. https://doi.org/10.1176/appi.books.9780890426821

National Institute of Mental Health. (2018). Bipolar Disorder. https://www.nimh.nih.gov/health/topics/bipolar-disorder/index.shtml

Centers for Disease Control and Prevention. (2018). Strategies for Preventing Suicide. https://www.cdc.gov/violenceprevention/pdf/suicide-strategic-direction-full-version-a.pdf

National Institute of Mental Health. (2018). Eating Disorders. https://www.nimh.nih.gov/health/topics/eating-disorders/index.shtml

Substance Abuse and Mental Health Services Administration. (2020). Prevention of Substance Abuse and Mental Illness. https://www.samhsa.gov/prevention

National Institute on Alcohol Abuse and Alcoholism. (2019). Understanding Alcohol Use Disorder. https://www.niaaa.nih.gov/publications/brochures-and-fact-sheets/understanding-alcohol-use-disorder

4

Nestler, E. J., Hyman, S. E., & Malenka, R. C. (2009). Molecular neuropharmacology: a foundation for clinical neuroscience (2nd ed.). New York: McGraw-Hill Medical.

Nirenberg, M. J., & Nestler, E. J. (2013). Neuroscience: Neurotransmitters and their receptors. In D. L. Longo, A. S. Fauci, D. L. Kasper, J. L. Jameson, & J. Loscalzo (Eds.), Harrison's principles of internal medicine (18th ed., pp. 2267-2284). New York: McGraw-Hill Medical.

Cools, R., Robinson, O. J., & Sahakian, B. (2008). Acute tryptophan depletion in healthy volunteers enhances punishment prediction but does not affect reward prediction. Neuropsychopharmacology, 33(9), 2291–2299. https://doi.org/10.1038/sj.npp.1301615

Craft, R. M., & Simon, E. J. (1978). Endorphins: A review of their analgesic and other pharmacological effects. Psychological Bulletin, 85(4), 910–940. https://doi.org/10.1037/0033-2909.85.4.910

Berridge, K. C., & Kringelbach, M. L. (2015). Pleasure systems in the brain. Neuron, 86(3), 646-664. https://doi.org/10.1016/j.neuron.2015.02.018

Blier, P., & Abbott, F. V. (2001). Putative mechanisms of action of antidepressant drugs in affective and anxiety disorders and pain. Journal of Psychiatry and Neuroscience, 26(1), 37-43.

Blier, P., & El Mansari, M. (2013). Serotonin and beyond: therapeutics for major depression. Philosophical Transactions of the Royal Society B: Biological Sciences, 368(1615), 20120536. https://doi.org/10.1098/rstb.2012.0536

Bryant, C. D., & Dunlop, J. (2019). Classical and novel opioid signaling in the regulation of reward behavior. Neuropharmacology, 146, 255-262. https://doi.org/10.1016/j.neuropharm.2018.09.012

Caspi, A., Sugden, K., Moffitt, T. E., Taylor, A., Craig, I. W., Harrington, H., McClay, J., Mill, J., Martin, J., Braithwaite, A., & Poulton, R. (2003). Influence of life stress on depression: moderation by a polymorphism in the 5-HTT gene. Science, 301(5631), 386-389. https://doi.org/10.1126/science.1083968

Cipriani, A., Furukawa, T. A., Salanti, G., Chaimani, A., Atkinson, L. Z., Ogawa, Y., Leucht, S., Ruhe, H. G., Turner, E. H., Higgins, J. P., Egger, M., Takeshima, N., Hayasaka, Y., Imai, H., Shinohara, K., Tajika, A., Ioannidis, J. P., Geddes, J. R., & Comparative Efficacy and Acceptability of 21 Antidepressant Drugs for the Acute Treatment of Adults With Major Depressive Disorder: A Systematic Review and Network Meta-Analysis. JAMA, 2018;319(9): 914-928. doi:10.1001/jama.2018.0245

Cools, R., Roberts, A. C., & Robbins, T. W. (2008). Serotoninergic regulation of emotional and behavioral control processes. Trends in cognitive sciences, 12(1), 31-40. https://doi.org/10.1016/j.tics.2007.10.001

Craft, L. L., & Perna, F. M. (2004). The benefits of exercise for the clinically depressed. Primary care companion to the Journal of clinical psychiatry, 6(3), 104-111. https://doi.org/10.4088/pcc.v06n0301

Craft, R. M., & Simon, E. J. (1978). Analgesia produced by injection of enkephalin into the lateral ventricle of the brain. Science, 200(4337), 1071-1073. https://doi.org/10.1126/science.347575

Dunbar, R. I., & Shultz, S. (2010). Bondedness and sociality. Behaviour,

Dunbar, R. I., Baron, R., Frangou, A., Pearce, E., van Leeuwen, E. J., Stow, J., Partridge, G., MacDonald, I., Barra, V., & van Vugt, M. (2012). Social laughter is correlated with an elevated pain threshold. Proceedings of the Royal Society B: Biological Sciences, 279(1731), 1161-1167. https://doi.org/10.1098/rspb.2011.1373

Grace, A. A. (2000). Gating of information flow within the limbic system and the pathophysiology of schizophrenia. Brain research Brain research reviews, 31(2-3), 330-341. https://doi.org/10.1016/s0165-0173(99)00042-5

Harmer, C. J. (2008). Serotonin and emotional processing: does it help explain antidepressant drug action? Neuropharmacology, 55(6), 1023-1028. https://doi.org/10.1016/j.neuropharm.2008.07.034

Harmer, C. J., & Cowen, P. J. (2013). "It's the way that you look at it"-a cognitive neuropsychological account of SSRI action in depression. Philosophical Transactions of the Royal Society B: Biological Sciences, 368(1615), 20120407. https://doi.org/10.1098/rstb.2012.0407

Koepp, M. J., Hammers, A., Lawrence, A. D., Asselin, M. C., Grasby, P. M., & Bench, C. J. (1998). Evidence for endogenous opioid release in the amygdala during positive emotion. NeuroImage, 8(4), 369-375. https://doi.org/10.1006/nimg.1998.0360

Kringelbach, M. L., & Berridge, K. C. (2010). The neuroscience of happiness and pleasure. Social research: an international quarterly, 77(2), 659-678. https://doi.org/10.1353/sor.2010.0002

Nestler, E. J., & Carlezon Jr, W. A. (2006). The mesolimbic dopamine reward circuit in depression. Biological psychiatry, 59(12), 1151-1159. https://doi.org/10.1016/j.biopsych.2005.09.018

Nummenmaa, L., Hirvonen, J., Parkkola, R., & Hietanen, J. K. (2016). Is emotional contagion special? An fMRI study on neural systems for affective and cognitive empathy. NeuroImage, 127, 494-501. https://doi.org/10.1016/j.neuroimage.2015.11.043

Pfeiffer, A., Brantl, V., Herz, A., & Emrich, H. M. (1986). Psychotomimesis mediated by $\varkappa$ opiate receptors. Science, 233(4765), 774-776. https://doi.org/10.1126/science.3016896

Schultz, W., Dayan, P., & Montague, P. R. (1997). A neural substrate of prediction and reward. Science, 275(5306), 1593-1599. https://doi.org/10.1126/science

Craft, L. L., & Perna, F. M. (2004). The benefits of exercise for the clinically depressed. Primary care companion to the Journal of clinical psychiatry, 6(3), 104-111. https://doi.org/10.4088/pcc.v06n0301

Craft, R. M., & Simon, E. J. (1978). Role of endorphins in mediating stress-induced analgesia. Science, 200(4341), 1086-1088. https://doi.org/10.1126/science.347575

Crockett, M. J., Clark, L., Tabibnia, G., Lieberman, M. D., & Robbins, T. W. (2008). Serotonin modulates behavioral reactions to unfairness. Science, 320(5884), 1739. https://doi.org/10.1126/science.1155577

Cools, R., Nakamura, K., & Daw, N. D. (2011). Serotonin and dopamine: unifying affective, activational, and decision functions. Neuropsychopharmacology, 36(1), 98-113. https://doi.org/10.1038/npp.2010.121

Zaki, J., & Williams, W. C. (2013). Interpersonal emotion regulation. Emotion, 13(5), 803-810. https://doi.org/10.1037/a0033840

Zubieta, J. K., Smith, Y. R., Bueller, J. A., Xu, Y., Kilbourn, M. R., Jewett, D. M., ... & Stohler, C. S. (2001). Regional mu opioid receptor regulation of sensory and affective dimensions of pain. Science, 293(5528), 311-315. https://doi.org/10.1126/science.1060952

5
Berridge, K. C., & Kringelbach, M. L. (2015). Pleasure systems in the brain. Neuron, 86(3), 646-664.
Kringelbach, M. L., & Berridge, K. C. (2010). Pleasures of the brain. New York: Oxford University Press.

6
Bentham, J. (1789). An Introduction to the Principles of Morals and Legislation. Clarendon Press.
Broad, C. D. (1952). Ethics and the History of Philosophy: Selected Books. Routledge.
Epicurus. (2008). The Essential Epicurus: Letters, Principal Doctrines, Vatican Sayings, and Fragments. Translated by Eugene O'Connor. B&N.
Mill, J. S. (1863). Utilitarianism. Longmans, Green, Reader, and Dyer.
Moore, G. E. (1903). Principia Ethica. Cambridge University Press.
Nussbaum, M. C. (1992). The Fragility of Goodness: Luck and Ethics in Greek Tragedy and Philosophy. Cambridge University Press.
Sandel, M. J. (2009). Justice: What's the Right Thing to Do? Farrar, Straus and Giroux.
Sartre, J. P. (1943). Being and Nothingness. Translated by Hazel E. Barnes. Philosophical Library.
Bentham, J. (1789). An Introduction to the Principles of Morals and Legislation. London: T. Payne.
Gavin, W. J. (2008). Augustine on Desire and the Meaning of Life. New York: Cambridge University Press.
Inwood, B. (2005). The Cambridge Companion to the Stoics. New York: Cambridge University Press.
Konstan, D. (2018). Epicurus. In E. N. Zalta (Ed.), The Stanford Encyclopedia of Philosophy (Summer 2018 ed.). Retrieved from https://plato.stanford.edu/archives/sum2018/entries/epicurus/.
Epicurus. (1994). The Epicurus Reader: Selected Writings and Testimonia. Hackett Publishing.
Nussbaum, M. C. (1994). The Therapy of Desire: Theory and Practice in Hellenistic Ethics. Princeton University Press.
Bentham, J. (1789). An introduction to the principles of morals and legislation. Printed for T. Payne and Son, at the Mews-Gate.
Mill, J. S. (1861). Utilitarianism. Longmans, Green, and Co.
Kahneman, D., Diener, E., & Schwarz, N. (1999). Well-being: The foundations of hedonic psychology. Russell Sage Foundation.
Wilson, T. D., & Gilbert, D. T. (2003). Affective forecasting. Advances in experimental social psychology, 35, 345-411.
Kahneman, D., & Tversky, A. (1979). Prospect theory: An analysis of decision under risk. Econometrica: Journal of the Econometric Society, 263-291.
Lyubomirsky, S. (2001). Why are some people happier than others? The role of cognitive and motivational processes in well-being. American psychologist, 56(3), 239-249.

Kringelbach, M. L., & Berridge, K. C. (2012). The Joyful Mind. Scientific American, 307(4), 44-49.

Stucki, S., & Rihs-Middel, M. (2017). The relationship between pleasure and well-being: a naturalistic study. Frontiers in Psychology, 8, 1964. https://doi.org/10.3389/fpsyg.2017.01964

Caprara, G. V., Steca, P., Gerbino, M., Paciello, M., & Vecchio, G. (2012). Looking for adolescents' well-being: self-efficacy beliefs as determinants of positive thinking and happiness. Epidemiology and psychiatric sciences, 21(3), 259-265. doi: 10.1017/S2045796011000891

Duckworth, A. L., Kirby, T. A., Tsukayama, E., Berstein, H., & Ericsson, K. A. (2012). Deliberate practice spells success: why grittier competitors triumph at the National Spelling Bee. Social Psychological and Personality Science, 3(2), 201-208. doi: 10.1177/1948550611416305

Flegal, K. M., Carroll, M. D., Kit, B. K., & Ogden, C. L. (2012). Prevalence of obesity and trends in the distribution of body mass index among US adults, 1999-2010. Journal of the American Medical Association, 307(5), 491-497. doi: 10.1001/jama.2012.39

Gentile, D. A. (2009). Pathological video-game use among youth ages 8 to 18: a national study. Psychological Science, 20(5), 594-602. doi: 10.1111/j.1467-9280.2009.02340.x

Hawkley, L. C., & Cacioppo, J. T. (2010). Loneliness matters: a theoretical and empirical review of consequences and mechanisms. Annals of Behavioral Medicine, 40(2), 218-227. doi: 10.1007/s12160-010

Lindemann, E. (2020). Overeating can lead to obesity, diabetes, and cardiovascular diseases. Journal of Nutrition Education and Behavior, 52(7), 753-758. https://doi.org/10.1016/j.jneb.2020.03.005

Koob, G. F. (2019). Substance abuse and addiction: A neurobiological perspective. Focus, 17(4), 371-377. https://doi.org/10.1176/appi.focus.17402

Biddle, S. J., Bennie, J. A., Bauman, A. E., Chau, J. Y., Dunstan, D., Owen, N., Stamatakis, E., & van Uffelen, J. G. (2019). Too much sitting and all-cause mortality: Is there a causal link? BMC Public Health, 19(1), 1-11. https://doi.org/10.1186/s12889-019-6903-3

Hawkley, L. C., & Cacioppo, J. T. (2010). Loneliness matters: A theoretical and empirical review of consequences and mechanisms. Annals of Behavioral Medicine, 40(2), 218-227. https://doi.org/10.1007/s12160-010-9210-8

Gentile, D. A. (2009). Pathological video-game use among youth ages 8 to 18: A national study. Psychological Science, 20(5), 594-602. https://doi.org/10.1111/j.1467-9280.2009.02340.x

American Psychiatric Association. (2013). Diagnostic and statistical manual of mental disorders (5th ed.). https://doi.org/10.1176/appi.books.9780890425596

Elster, J. (2019). Alchemies of the mind: Rationality and the emotions (2nd ed.). Cambridge University Press. https://doi.org/10.1017/9781108672387

Koob, G. F. (2019). Substance abuse and addiction: A neurobiological perspective. Focus, 17(4), 371-377. https://doi.org/10.1176/appi.focus.17402

Laukka, P., Juslin, P. N., & Bresin, R. (2021). Pleasure and emotions: Music, movement, and the brain. In S. S. Schiffman & J. H. Graham (Eds.), Sensation and perception (5th ed., pp. 435-466). SAGE Publications. https://doi.org/10.1177/0963721420946186

7

Kasser, T. (2002). The high price of materialism. MIT Press.

Anderson, C. A., Berkowitz, L., Donnerstein, E., Huesmann, L. R., Johnson, J. D., Linz, D., Malamuth, N. M., & Wartella, E. (2003). The influence of media violence on youth. Psychological Science in the Public Interest, 4(3), 81-110.

Kahn, P. H. (1999). The human relationship with nature: Development and culture. MIT Press.

Post, S. G. (2005). Altruism, happiness, and health: It's good to be good. International Journal of Behavioral Medicine, 12(2), 66-77.

Csikszentmihalyi, M., & Csikszentmihalyi, I. S. (1988). Optimal experience: Psychological studies of flow in consciousness. Cambridge University Press.

Bauer, K. W., & Hamm, M. W. (2004). The French paradox: Eating for pleasure, health, and pleasure. Journal of the American Dietetic Association, 104(11), 1718-1725.

Bukhari, M. I., Muslim, A., Abu-Dawud, S., & Al-Tirmidhi, A. (1994). Sahih Bukhari. Lahore, Pakistan: Islamic Publishers.

Connor, J., Pihl, R. O., & Scholey, A. (2016). The moderating effect of masculinity/femininity on the relation between alcohol consumption and cognitive performance. Addiction Research & Theory, 24(1), 15-22.

Csikszentmihalyi, M., & Rochberg-Halton, E. (1981). The meaning of things: Domestic symbols and the self. Cambridge, UK: Cambridge University Press.

Counihan, C., & Van Esterik, P. (2013). Food and culture: A reader. New York, NY: Routledge.

de Visser, R. O., McDonnell, E. J., Newell, C., & Gibson, A. (2017). 'It's just not part of the culture': Young lesbian and bisexual women's experiences of negotiating alcohol-related risks. International Journal of Drug Policy, 49, 38-46.

DeLamater, J., & Hyde, J. S. (1998). Essentialism vs. social constructionism in the study of human sexuality.

Journal of Sex Research, 35(1), 10-18.

Diener, E., Oishi, S., & Tay, L. (2017). Advances in subjective well-being research. Nature Human Behaviour, 1(8), 1-10.

Hansen, K. T., Lambert, N. M., & Forman, E. M. (2015). The effect of positive mood induction on working memory and cognitive control. Psychology of Consciousness: Theory, Research, and Practice, 2(2), 145-152.

Herbenick, D., Bowling, J., Fu, T. C., Guerra-Reyes, L., Sanders, S. A., Dodge, B., & Fortenberry, J. D. (2018). Sexual diversity in the United States: Results from a nationally representative probability sample of adult women and men. PLoS One, 13(1), e0181198.

Jaworowska, A., Blackham, T., & Davies, I. G. (2013). The effect of eating breakfast cereal on cognition and mood in children and adolescents. Frontiers in Human Neuroscience, 7, 425.

Kashdan, T. B., Ferssizidis, P., Collins, R. L., & Muraven, M. (2010). Emotion differentiation as resilience against excessive alcohol use: An ecological momentary assessment in underage social drinkers. Psychological Science, 21(9), 1341-1347.

Kittler, P. G., & Sucher, K. P. (2017). Food and culture. Cengage Learning.

Lambert, N. M., & Brown, T. L. (2015). The hedonic psychology of artisanal food and beverages. In Artisanal food and beverage marketing (pp. 1-13). Routledge.

Lau-Barraco, C., & Linden-Carmichael, A. N. (2017). Drinking motives mediate cultural differences but not gender differences in college students' alcohol use. Journal of Studies on Alcohol and Drugs, 78

Crossman, J. (2008). Sports in society: Issues and controversies (10th ed.). McGraw-Hill.

Fischler, C. (1988). Food, self, and identity. Social Science Information, 27(2), 275-292.

Fukushima, S. (2005). Wabi-sabi aesthetics: A paradigmatic shift? Human Studies, 28(3), 303-317.

Gagnon, J. H., & Simon, W. (2005). Sexual conduct: The social sources of human sexuality (2nd ed.). Aldine

Zahavi, D. (2011). Self and other: Exploring subjectivity, empathy, and shame. Oxford University Press.

Chua, S., & Chang, S. (2016). Sex and culture. In J. L. Matsumoto, L. Hwang, & M. Yoo (Eds.), Culture and psychology (pp. 285-304). Cengage Learning.

Herek, G. M., & McLemore, K. A. (2013). Sexual stigma. In A. Goldberg (Ed.), The Sage encyclopedia of LGBTQ studies (pp. 761-764). Sage.

Henderson, J. T., & Kim, C. (2016). Sexual health education. In K. Glanz, B. K. Rimer, & K. Viswanath (Eds.), Health behavior: Theory, research, and practice (5th ed., pp. 527-543). Jossey-Bass.

Herbenick, D., Reece, M., Schick, V., Sanders, S. A., Dodge, B., & Fortenberry, J. D. (2017). Sexual behavior in the United States: Results from a national probability sample of men and women ages 14-94. The Journal of Sexual Medicine, 14(7), 857-868.

Wood, J. T., Schmader, T., & Martens, A. (2020). Gendered communication in cultural context. Oxford University Press.

Crossman, J. (2008). Sports in society: Issues and controversies (10th ed.). McGraw-Hill.

Ito, T. A., & Cacioppo, J. T. (2018). The influence of cultural background on the neural response to pleasant stimuli. Social Cognitive and Affective Neuroscience, 13(3), 239-249.

Lonsdale, A. J., & North, A. C. (2011). Why do we listen to music? A uses and gratifications analysis. British Journal of Psychology, 102(1), 108-134.

Provencher, V., Polivy, J., Herman, C. P., & Tapper, K. (2012). Caloric estimation of healthy and unhealthy foods in normal-weight, overweight and obese participants. Appetite, 58(1), 26-33.

Zahavi, D. (2011). Self and other: Exploring subjectivity, empathy, and shame. Oxford University Press.

Abusharaf, R. (2006). Female genital cutting: Cultural conflict in the global community. Johns Hopkins University Press.

Dissanayake, E. (2000). Art and intimacy: How the arts began. University of Washington Press.

Foucault, M. (1984). The history of sexuality, Volume 1: An introduction. Vintage.

Kittler, P. G., & Sucher, K. P. (2007). Food and culture. Cengage Learning.

Mintz, S. W. (1985). Sweetness and power: The place of sugar in modern history. Penguin.

Connor, J., You, R. Q., & Casswell, S. (2016). Alcohol-related harm in Asia and the Pacific: A review of the evidence. Drug and Alcohol Review, 35(1), 1-11.

Lau-Barraco, C., & Linden-Carmichael, A. N. (2017). Drinking motives and social-contextual factors in predicting college student drinking. Journal of American College Health, 65(4), 276-283.

Livingston, M. (2016). Alcohol availability and harms in the Pacific Islands. In M. Anderson & B. R. Room (Eds.), The impact of alcohol consumption on societies: A research agenda (pp. 243-256). Springer.

Scheinbaum, S., Fleming, K., & Kedia, S. (2016). Drinking cultures and alcohol policies. In M. Anderson & B. R. Room (Eds.), The impact of alcohol consumption on societies: A research agenda (pp. 259-278). Springer.

Scheffels, J., & Ottersen, T. (2015). The Norwegian alcohol culture: Drinking and drunkenness in the Norwegian public debate. International Journal of Drug Policy, 26(11), 1131-1139.

de Visser, R. O., McDonnell, E. J., & Rich, A. (2017). Sex and HIV: Perceptions of sexual risk in a representative sample of adults in England and Wales. AIDS Care, 29(10), 1255-1262.

DeLamater, J., & Hyde, J. S. (1998). Essentialism vs. social constructionism in the study of human sexuality. Journal of Sex Research, 35(1), 10-18.

Herbenick, D., Reece, M., Hensel, D., Sanders, S. A., Jozkowski, K. N., Fortenberry, J. D., & Gershel, L. (2018). Sexual communication among college students: Comparisons across a decade. Journal of Sex Research, 55(5), 557-573.

Levy, V., Aung, T., Feldblum, P. J., Winn, T., & Dallabetta, G. (2016). Condom use among Myanmar migrant workers in Thailand. AIDS and Behavior, 20(6), 1186-1193.

Wight, D., Fullerton, D., & Aitchison, C. (2016). Six steps in quality intervention development (6SQuID). Journal of Epidemiology and Community Health, 70(5), 520-525.

Yang, X., Lu, H., & Stanton, B. (2010). Culturally appropriate sexual health interventions for Asian adolescents: A review of literature. Sex Education, 10(4), 375-392.

Zhang, T., Han, L., Huang, Y., Cui, W., & Tulloch, H. E. (2016). Understanding risky sexual behavior among male and female adolescents in developing countries: A review of the literature. AIDS and Behavior, 20(10), 2193-2214.

Bauer, J., & Hamm, M. W. (2004). Health and pleasure in consumers' dietary food choices: Individual differences in the consideration of sensory and health cues. Appetite, 43(3), 285-296.

Counihan, C., & Van Esterik, P. (2013). Food and culture: A reader. Routledge.

Jaworowska, A., Blackham, T., Davies, I. G., & Stevenson, L. (2013). Nutritional challenges and health implications of takeaway and fast food. Nutrition Reviews, 71(5), 310-318.

Kittler, P. G., & Sucher, K. P. (2017). Food and culture. Cengage Learning.

Mintz, S. W., & Du Bois, C. M. (2002). The anthropology of food and eating. Annual Review of Anthropology, 31(1), 99-119.

Sutton, D. E. (2001). Remembrance of repasts: An anthropology of food and memory. Berg.

Wahlqvist, M. L. (2011). The Asian paradox: More plants, less breast cancer. World Review of Nutrition and Dietetics, 101, 130-140.

Bauer, K. W., & Hamm, M. W. (2004). Evaluation of a nutrition intervention for women residents of two religious communities. Journal of Nutrition Education and Behavior, 36(5), 263–271. https://doi.org/10.1016/s1499-4046(06)60267-1

Csikszentmihalyi, M., & Rochberg-Halton, E. (1981). The meaning of things: Domestic symbols and the self. Cambridge University Press.

Lambert, Y., & Brown, S. (2015). The pleasures of consumption and the consumption of pleasures: Introduction to the special issue. Journal of Consumer Research, 42(6), 931–947. https://doi.org/10.1086/682112

Wahlqvist, M. L. (2011). Food culture: Relevance and application. Asia Pacific Journal of Clinical Nutrition, 20(4), 423–430. https://doi.org/10.6133/apjcn.2011.20.4.03

Bauer, D., & Hamm, R. (2004). Cultural differences in eating behaviors: A review of research on Americans and Europeans. Eating and Weight Disorders, 9(2), 97-103.

Bukhari, M., Muslim, A., Abu-Dawud, S., & Al-Tirmidhi, A. (1994). Sahih al-Bukhari. Darussalam.

DeLamater, J. D., & Hyde, J. S. (1998). Essentialism versus social constructionism in the study of human sexuality. Journal of Sex Research, 35(1), 10-18.

Solecki, S. (2008). Cultural differences in alcohol use. Substance Use & Misuse, 43(3-4), 354-357.

Wahlqvist, M. L. (2011). Food habits and culture in the Asia Pacific region: A role in the prevention of chronic diseases. Asia Pacific Journal of Clinical Nutrition, 20(3), 447-455.

Yang, X., Lu, H., & Stanton, B. (2010). Understanding HIV-related stigma and discrimination in a "blameless" population. AIDS Education and Prevention, 22(2), 170-182.

Christofides, E., Muise, A., & Desmarais, S. (2009). Risky disclosures on Facebook: The effect of having a bad experience on willingness to disclose. Journal of Social and Personal Relationships, 26(5), 701-721.

Cohen, S. (2015). The pleasure of food: The history of gastronomy and the cultural evolution of taste. Rowman & Littlefield.

Soper, K. (2017). Alternative hedonism, cultural theory and the role of aesthetic revisioning. Cultural Studies, 31(2-3), 369-389.

Tsai, M. (2019). Confucianism and the culture of happiness: An overview. Journal of Happiness Studies, 20(6), 1731-1755.

Wilson, D., & Vanston, C. (2018). Social inequality, class and the commodification of leisure. In The Routledge Handbook of Leisure Studies (pp. 107-118). Routledge.

Bianchi, C., Kogg, B., & Wittmer, A. (2018). The impact of luxury consumption on environmental sustainability. Journal of Business Research, 86, 340-348.

Bourdieu, P. (1984). Distinction: A social critique of the judgement of taste. Harvard University Press.

Ferguson, C. J., Coulson, M., & Barnett, J. (2017). Psychological profiles of players of violent video games: Analysis of the relationship between immersion, interpersonal aggression, and desensitization. Journal of Interpersonal Violence, 32(19), 2985-3008.

Flegal, K. M., Kruszon-Moran, D., Carroll, M. D., Fryar, C. D., & Ogden, C. L. (2012). Trends in obesity among adults in the United States, 2005 to 2014. Journal of the American Medical Association, 315(21), 2284-2291.

Gössling, S., Scott, D., & Hall, C. M. (2020). Tourism and water: Interactions, impacts and challenges. Channel View Publications.

National Institute on Drug Abuse. (2021). Drug misuse and addiction. Retrieved from https://www.drugabuse.gov/publications/drugfacts/drug-misuse-addiction

Cacioppo, J. T., Cacioppo, S., Capitanio, J. P., & Cole, S. W. (2015). The neuroendocrinology of social isolation. Annual Review of Psychology, 66, 733-767.

Duffy, B. (2018). Unequal pleasures: Exploring the social determinants of pleasure in the global south. Feminist Theory, 19(1), 49-68.

Friedman, S. R., Mateu-Gelabert, P., Sandoval, M., Hagan, H., & Des Jarlais, D. C. (2018). Positive deviance control-case life history: A method to develop grounded hypotheses about successful long-term avoidance of infection. BMC Public Health, 18(1), 434.

Hawkins, K. (2020). Sexual pleasure and exploitation: The language of consent in prostitution policy debates. Sexualities, 23(1-2), 53-71.

Hochschild, A. R. (2012). The managed heart: Commercialization of human feeling. University of California Press.

Karpowitz, D. (2017). Pleasure and power: The politics of enjoyment. American Political Science Review, 111(3), 487-498.

Zhang, Y., Zhang, L., & Li, X. (2021). Effects of recreational activities on social bonding: A systematic review and meta-analysis. Journal of Leisure Research, 52(1), 1-16.

Crawford, M. (1984). The social construction of male and female sexuality. In J. H. Pleck & J. H. Hershberger (Eds.), The male sexual experience (pp. 9-36). Wadsworth.

Crossick, G. (2005). Pleasures and pastimes in Victorian Britain. Oxford University Press.

Giddens, A. (2013). The consequences of modernity. John Wiley & Sons.

Jackson, S. (2016). The social shaping of pleasure: Exploring the socio-cultural contexts of pleasure. European Journal of Cultural Studies, 19(5), 461-478.

Kivinen, M. (2011). Culture and pleasure: Towards a sociology of enjoyment. Routledge.

Kwon, H. (2011). Cultural history of pleasure in modern Korea. Journal of Korean Studies, 16(2), 215-240.

Skeggs, B. (2005). The moral economy of person production: The class relations of self-performance on "reality" television. The Sociological Review, 53(2_suppl), 104-120.

Bourdieu, P. (1984). Distinction: A social critique of the judgement of taste. Harvard University Press.

Braun, V., Gavey, N., & McPhillips, K. (2017). The 'fair deal'? Unpacking accounts of reciprocity in heterosexual oral sex. Sexualities, 20(1-2), 29-48.

Hochschild, A. R. (1983). The managed heart: Commercialization of human feeling. University of California Press.

Skeggs, B. (1997). Formations of class and gender: Becoming respectable. Sage.

Cacioppo, J. T., Cacioppo, S., & Capitanio, J. P. (2015). Toward a neurology of loneliness. Psychological Bulletin, 140(6), 1464-1504. https://doi.org/10.1037/bul0000021

Giddens, A. (2013). The transformation of intimacy: Sexuality, love, and eroticism in modern societies. John Wiley & Sons.

Hochschild, A. R. (1983). The managed heart: Commercialization of human feeling. University of California Press.

Hochschild, A. R. (2012). The outsourced self: Intimate life in market times. Metropolitan Books.

Jackson, S. (2016). The cultural politics of emotion. Edinburgh University Press.

Skeggs, B. (1997). Formations of class and gender: Becoming respectable. Sage.

Amabile, T. M. (1996). Creativity in context: Update to the social psychology of creativity. Westview Press.

Bedeian, A. G. (2003). Workplace pleasure and power: A reconsideration of the managerial prerogative. Organization, 10(2), 309-327.

Csikszentmihalyi, M. (1990). Flow: The psychology of optimal experience. Harper & Row.

Maslach, C., Schaufeli, W. B., & Leiter, M. P. (2001). Job burnout. Annual Review of Psychology, 52, 397-422.

Steel, P. (2007). The nature of procrastination: A meta-analytic and theoretical review of quintessential self-regulatory failure. Psychological Bulletin, 133(1), 65-94.

Anderson, C. A., Berkowitz, L., Donnerstein, E., Huesmann, L. R., Johnson, J. D., Linz, D., ... & Wartella, E. (2003). The influence of media violence on youth. Psychological Science in the Public Interest, 4(3), 81-110.

Cacioppo, S., Cacioppo, J. T., & Decety, J. (2015). Social neuroscience: Challenges and opportunities in the study of complex behavior. Annals of the New York Academy of Sciences, 1337, 1-13.

Csikszentmihalyi, M., & Csikszentmihalyi, I. S. (1988). Optimal experience: Psychological studies of flow in consciousness. Cambridge University Press.

Diener, E., Suh, E. M., Lucas, R. E., & Smith, H. L. (1999). Subjective well-being: Three decades of progress.

Psychological Bulletin, 125(2), 276-302.

Fredrickson, B. L. (2004). The broaden-and-build theory of positive emotions. Philosophical Transactions of the Royal Society B: Biological Sciences

Csikszentmihalyi, M., & Rochberg-Halton, E. (1981). The meaning of things: Domestic symbols and the self. Cambridge University Press.

Bedeian, A. G. (2003). Waking up to the realities of power in organizations. Journal of Management, 29(3), 359-360.

Bourdieu, P. (1984). Distinction: A social critique of the judgment of taste. Harvard University Press.

Cacioppo, J. T., Fowler, J. H., & Christakis, N. A. (2015). Alone in the crowd: The structure and spread of loneliness in a large social network. Journal of Personality and Social Psychology, 109(4), 746-761.

Csikszentmihalyi, M. (1990). Flow: The psychology of optimal experience. Harper & Row.

Fredrickson, B. L. (2004). Gratitude, like other positive emotions, broadens and builds. In R. A. Emmons & M. E. McCullough (Eds.), The psychology of gratitude (pp. 145-166). Oxford University Press.

Grunert, K. G. (2005). Food quality and safety: Consumer perception and demand. European Review of Agricultural Economics, 32(3), 369-391.

Hochschild, A. R. (2012). The managed heart: Commercialization of human feeling. University of California Press.

Kasser, T. (2002). The high price of materialism. MIT Press.

Steel, P. (2007). The nature of procrastination: A meta-analytic and theoretical review of quintessential self-regulatory failure. Psychological Bulletin, 133(1), 65-94.

Berridge, K. C., & Kringelbach, M. L. (2015). Pleasure systems in the brain. Neuron, 86(3), 646-664.

Fishbein, M., & Ajzen, I. (2010). Predicting and changing behavior: The reasoned action approach. Psychology Press.

Knobloch-Westerwick, S., & Meng, J. (2009). Looking the other way: Selective exposure to attitude-consistent and counterattitudinal political information. Communication Research, 36(3), 426-448.

Kringelbach, M. L., & Berridge, K. C. (2010). Pleasures of the brain. Oxford University Press.

Belk, R. W., & Coon, G. S. (1993). Gift giving as agapic love: An alternative to the exchange paradigm based on dating experiences. Journal of Consumer Research, 20(3), 393-417.

Bicchieri, C. (2016). Norms in the wild: How to diagnose, measure, and change social norms. Oxford University Press.

Cialdini, R. B., & Trost, M. R. (1998). Social influence: Social norms, conformity, and compliance. In D. T. Gilbert, S. T. Fiske, & G. Lindzey (Eds.), The handbook of social psychology (pp. 151-192). McGraw-Hill.

Crane, D., & Bovone, L. (2006). Fashion and identity in America: The impact of gender and social class. Routledge.

Giddens, A. (1992). The transformation of intimacy: Sexuality, love and eroticism in modern societies. Polity Press.

Hall, E. T. (1966). The hidden dimension. Doubleday.

Jackman, M. R., & Crane, M. (1986). "Some of my best friends are…": Interracial friendships and whites' racial attitudes. Public Opinion Quarterly, 50(4), 459-486.

Lifton, R. J. (2000). The protean self: Human resilience in an age of fragmentation. Basic Books.

Mead, G. H. (193

Mead, G. H. (1934). Mind, self, and society. University of Chicago Press.

Milgram, S. (1974). Obedience to authority: An experimental view. Harper & Row.

Ridgeway, C. L., & Correll, S. J. (2004). Unpacking the gender system: A theoretical perspective on gender beliefs and social relations. Gender & Society, 18(4), 510-531.

Turkle, S. (2011). Alone together: Why we expect more from technology and less from each other. Basic Books.

D'Amico, E. J., & Jones, K. L. (2019). Trends in marijuana use among college students in the United States. Frontiers in Psychiatry, 10, 1-5.

Fishbein, M., & Ajzen, I. (2010). Predicting and changing behavior: The reasoned action approach. Psychology Press.

Knobloch-Westerwick, S., & Meng, J. (2009). Looking the other way: Selective exposure to attitude-consistent and counterattitudinal political information. Communication Research, 36(3), 426-448.

Berridge, K. C., & Kringelbach, M. L. (2015). Pleasure systems in the brain. Neuron, 86(3), 646-664.

Bicchieri, C. (2016). Norms in the wild: How to diagnose, measure, and change social norms. Oxford University Press.

Cialdini, R. B., & Trost, M. R. (1998). Social influence: Social norms, conformity and compliance. In D. T. Gilbert, S. T. Fiske, & G. Lindzey (Eds.), The handbook of social psychology (Vol. 2, pp. 151-192). Oxford, England: Oxford University Press.

Fishbein, M., & Ajzen, I. (2010). Predicting and changing behavior: The reasoned action approach. Psychology Press.

Knobloch-Westerwick, S., & Meng, J. (2009). Looking the other way: Selective exposure to attitude

Berridge, K. C., & Kringelbach, M. L. (2015). Pleasure systems in the brain. Neuron, 86(3), 646-664.

Cialdini, R. B., & Trost, M. R. (1998). Social influence: Social norms, conformity and compliance. In D. T. Gilbert, S. T. Fiske, & G. Lindzey (Eds.), The handbook of social psychology (Vol. 2, pp. 151-192). Oxford, England: Oxford University Press.

Fishbein, M., & Ajzen, I. (2010). Predicting and changing behavior: The reasoned action approach. Psychology Press.

Knobloch-Westerwick, S., & Meng, J. (2009). Looking the other way: Selective exposure to attitude-consistent and counterattitudinal political information. Communication Research, 36(3), 426-448.

Bauer, K. W., & Hamm, M. W. (2004). Evaluation of a statewide environmental intervention to increase fruit and vegetable consumption. American Journal of Health Promotion, 18(3), 190-193.

Belk, R. W., & Coon, N. A. (1993). Gift giving as agapic love: An alternative to the exchange paradigm based on dating experiences. Journal of Consumer Research, 20(3), 393-417.

Berridge, K. C., & Kringelbach, M. L. (2015). Pleasure systems in the brain. Neuron, 86(3), 646-664.

Bicchieri, C. (2016). Norms in the Wild: How to Diagnose, Measure, and Change Social Norms. Oxford University Press.

Bukhari, M. I., Muslim, I., Abu-Dawud, S., & Al-Tirmidhi, M. (1994). Sahih Bukhari. Islamic Book Service.

Cialdini, R. B., & Trost, M. R. (1998). Social influence: Social norms, conformity and compliance. In D. T. Gilbert, S. T. Fiske, & G. Lindzey (Eds.), The handbook of social psychology (4th ed., Vol. 2, pp. 151-192). McGraw-Hill.

Connor, J. P., Haber, P. S., Hall, W. D., Jarrett, M., & Toumbourou, J. W. (2016). Young people's use of alcohol and their attitudes towards alcohol advertising. Australian and New Zealand Journal of Public Health, 40(6), 580-586.

Crane, D., & Bovone, L. (2006). Fashion and its social agendas: Class, gender, and identity in clothing. University of Chicago Press.

Csikszentmihalyi, M., & Rochberg-Halton, E. (1981). The meaning of things: Domestic symbols and the self. Cambridge University Press.

D'Amico, E. J., & Jones, K. L. (2019). Promoting change in the alcohol use behavior of American Indians and Alaska Natives. American Journal of Psychiatry, 176(11), 853-862.

DeLamater, J., & Hyde, J. S. (1998). Essentialism vs. social constructionism in the study of human sexuality. The Journal of Sex Research, 35(1), 10-18.

Fishbein, M., & Ajzen, I. (2010). Predicting and changing behavior: The reasoned action approach. Psychology Press.

Giddens, A. (1992). The transformation of intimacy: Sexuality, love, and eroticism in modern societies. Stanford University Press.

Hall, E. T. (1966). The hidden dimension. Doubleday.

Herbenick, D., Reece, M., Schick, V., Sanders, S. A., Dodge, B., & Fortenberry, J. D. (2018). Sexual behavior in the United States: Results from a national probability sample of men and women ages 14-94. The Journal of Sexual Medicine, 15(3), 319-328.

Jackman, M. R., & Crane, M. (1986). "Some of my best friends are…": Interracial friendships and whites' racial attitudes. Public Opinion Quarterly, 50(4), 459-486.

Knobloch-Westerwick, S., & Meng, J.

Bicchieri, C. (2016). Norms in the Wild: How to Diagnose, Measure, and Change Social Norms. Oxford University Press.

Belk, R. W., & Coon, G. S. (1993). Gift giving as agapic love: An alternative to the exchange paradigm based on dating experiences. Journal of Consumer Research, 20(3), 393-417.

Cialdini, R. B., & Trost, M. R. (1998). Social influence: Social norms, conformity and compliance. In The handbook of social psychology (Vol. 2, pp. 151-192).

Crane, D., & Bovone, L. (2006). Fashion and its social agendas: Class, gender, and identity in clothing. University of Chicago Press.

D'Amico, E. J., & Jones, C. M. (2019). Trends in marijuana use among adults in the United States, 2016–2017. JAMA, 322(16), 1619-1621.

Fishbein, M., & Ajzen, I. (2010). Predicting and changing behavior: The reasoned action approach. Psychology Press.

Giddens, A. (1992). The transformation of intimacy: Sexuality, love, and eroticism in modern societies. Stanford University Press.

Hall, E. T. (1966). The hidden dimension. Anchor Books.

Jackman, M. R., & Crane, M. (1986). "Some of my best friends are…": Interracial friendship and whites' racial attitudes. Public Opinion Quarterly, 50(4), 459-486.

Knobloch-Westerwick, S., & Meng, J. (2009). Looking the other way: Selective exposure to attitude-consistent and counterattitudinal political information. Communication Research, 36(3), 426-448.

Kringelbach, M. L., & Berridge, K. C. (2010). The joy of hedonism: Why dopamine and hedonic enjoyment are central in motivating human behavior. In Pleasures of the brain (pp. 1-15). Oxford University Press.

Lifton, R. J. (2000). The protean self: Human resilience in an age of fragmentation. Basic Books.

Mead, M. (1934). Culture and commitment. American Journal of Sociology, 39(6), 826-847.

Milgram, S. (1974). Obedience to authority: An experimental view. Harper & Row.

Ridgeway, C. L., & Correll, S. J. (2004). Unpacking the gender system: A theoretical perspective on gender beliefs and social relations. Gender & Society, 18(4), 510-531.

Turkle, S. (2011). Alone together: Why we expect more from technology and less from each other. Basic Books.

8

Baumeister, R. F., & Tierney, J. (2011). Willpower: Rediscovering the greatest human strength. Penguin.

Burrow, A. L., & Wegner, D. M. (2016). Mindful pleasurable consumption: mindfulness enhances enjoyment of pleasurable experiences. Journal of Consumer Psychology, 26(1), 114-127.

Du Plessis, E., & Hensher, M. A. (2015). Hedonic adaptation and the dark side of pleasure: Evidence from gambling behavior. Journal of Behavioral and Experimental Economics, 56, 1-11.

Vohs, K. D., & Baumeister, R. F. (Eds.). (2011). Handbook of self-regulation: Research, theory, and applications. Guilford Press.

Koob, G. F., & Volkow, N. D. (2010). Neurocircuitry of addiction. Neuropsychopharmacology, 35(1), 217-238.

Nestler, E. J. (2005). Is there a common molecular pathway for addiction? Nature Neuroscience, 8(11), 1445-1449.

Volkow, N. D., & Li, T. K. (2004). Drug addiction: The neurobiology of disrupted self-control. Trends in Molecular Medicine, 10(5), &-189.

Wise, R. A. (1996). Addictive drugs and brain stimulation reward. Annual Review of Psychology, 47, 1-32.

American Psychiatric Association. (2013). Diagnostic and Statistical Manual of Mental Disorders, Fifth Edition. Washington, DC: American Psychiatric Association.

National Institute on Drug Abuse. (2018). The Science of Drug Abuse and Addiction: The Basics. https://www.drugabuse.gov/publications/drugfacts/science-drug-abuse-addiction-basics

National Council on Problem Gambling. (2021). The Impact of Problem Gambling on the Gambler. https://www.ncpgambling.org/help-treatment/impact-on-the-individual/

Volkow, N. D., Koob, G. F., & McLellan, A. T. (2016). Neurobiologic advances from the brain disease model of addiction. New England Journal of Medicine, 374(4), 363-371. https://doi.org/10.1056/NEJMra1511480

Frederick, S., & Loewenstein, G. (1999). Hedonic adaptation. In D. Kahneman, E. Diener, & N. Schwarz (Eds.), Well-being: The foundations of hedonic psychology (pp. 302-329). Russell Sage Foundation.

Twenge, J. M., & Campbell, W. K. (2009). The narcissism epidemic: Living in the age of entitlement. Free Press.

Berridge, K.C., & Kringelbach, M.L. (2015). Pleasure systems in the brain. Neuron, 86(3), 646-664. https://doi.org/10.1016/j.neuron.2015.02.018

Frederick, S., & Loewenstein, G. (1999). Hedonic adaptation. In D. Kahneman, E. Diener, & N. Schwarz (Eds.), Well-being: The foundations of hedonic psychology (pp. 302-329). Russell Sage Foundation.

Twenge, J. M., & Campbell, W. K. (2009). The narcissism epidemic

American Psychological Association. (2018). Financial problems and mental health.

Baumeister, R. F., & Tierney, J. (2011). Willpower: Rediscovering the greatest human strength. Penguin.

Center for Substance Abuse Research. (2016). The effects of substance abuse on families.

Kasser, T., & Ryan, R. M. (1996). Further examining the American dream: Differential correlates of intrinsic and extrinsic goals. Personality and Social Psychology Bulletin, 22(3), 280-287.

National Institute on Drug Abuse. (2018). The health effects of drug abuse.

National Institute of Mental Health. (2019). Substance abuse and mental health.

9

Park, C. L., Koenig, H. G., & Park, N. (2015). Handbook of Religion and Health. Oxford University Press.

Underwood, L. G., Teresi, J. A., & Gatz, M. (2002). Spirituality and Well-Being in Late Life. The Gerontologist, 42(6), 763-770.

Baumeister, R. F., & Leary, M. R. (1995). The need to belong: Desire for interpersonal attachments as a fundamental human motivation. Psychological Bulletin, 117(3), 497-529.

Fredrickson, B. L. (2013). Positive emotions broaden and build. Advances in Experimental Social Psychology, 47, 1-53.

Rumi, J. (13th century). Masnavi.

The Holy Bible (New International Version). (1984). Grand Rapids, MI: Zondervan.

The Four Noble Truths. (n.d.). Retrieved March 14, 2023, from https://www.buddhanet.net/e-learning/history/buddhism/4truths.htm

Csikszentmihalyi, M. (1990). Flow: The psychology of optimal experience. Harper & Row.

Fink, A., & Benedek, M. (2014). EEG alpha power and creative ideation. Neuroscience & Biobehavioral Reviews, 44, 111-123.

Maslow, A. H. (1964). Religions, values, and peak-experiences. Ohio State University Press.

Newberg, A. B., & Waldman, M. R. (2017). The spiritual brain: A neuroscientist's case for the existence of the soul. HarperOne.

Vollenweider, F. X., & Kometer, M. (2010). The neurobiology of psychedelic drugs: Implications for the treatment of mood disorders. Nature Reviews Neuroscience, 11(9), 642-651.

Epicurus. (n.d.). In Stanford Encyclopedia of Philosophy. Retrieved from https://plato.stanford.edu/entries/epicurus/

Feuerstein, G. (1998). The Shambhala Guide to Tantra. Shambhala Publications.

Hinduism Today. (2015, March). Tantra: The Path of Ecstasy. Retrieved from https://www.hinduismtoday.com/modules/smartsection/item.php?itemid=5637

10

Baumeister, R. F. (1991). Meanings of life. Guilford Press.

Brown, B. (2010). The gifts of imperfection: Let go of who you think you're supposed to be and embrace who you are. Hazelden Publishing.

Kringelbach, M. L., & Berridge, K. C. (2010). The neuroscience of pleasure, reward, and addiction. In Oxford Handbook of Affective Sciences (pp. 637-657). Oxford University Press.

Ryan, R. M., & Deci, E. L. (2017). Self-determination theory: Basic psychological needs in motivation, development, and wellness. Guilford Press.

Dissanayake, E. (2014). What is art for? University of Washington Press.

Langer, S. K. (1957). Philosophy in a new key: A study in the symbolism of reason, rite, and art. Harvard University Press.

Csikszentmihalyi, M. (1990). Flow: The psychology of optimal experience. Harper Perennial.

Kant, I. (1790). Critique of Judgment.

Schopenhauer, A. (1851). The World as Will and Representation.

Nietzsche, F. (1872). The Birth of Tragedy.

Dewey, J. (1934). Art as Experience.

Pine, B. J., & Gilmore, J. H. (1998). Welcome to the experience economy. Harvard business review, 76(4), 97-105.

Norman, D. A. (2004). Emotional design: Why we love (or hate) everyday things. Basic Civitas Books.

Hassenzahl, M. (2010). Experience design: Technology for all the right reasons. Morgan Kaufmann.

Norman, D. A. (2013). The design of everyday things: Revised and expanded edition. Basic Books.

Kim, Y., Lee, K. C., & Choi, H. J. (2011). The effects of hedonic and utilitarian value on user satisfaction and loyalty in the mobile context. Information Systems Journal, 21(6), 475-496.

11

Kringelbach, M. L. (2019). The pleasure center: Trust your animal instincts. Oxford University Press.

Berridge, K. C., & Kringelbach, M. L. (2015). Pleasure systems in the brain. Neuron, 86(3), 646-664.

Schellekens, A. F., & Kringelbach, M. L. (2016). The pleasure of social interactions. Nature Human Behaviour, 1(8), 0051.

Fredrickson, B. L. (2001). The role of positive emotions in positive psychology: The broaden-and-build theory of positive emotions. American Psychologist, 56(3), 218-226.

Seligman, M. E. P. (2011). Flourish: A visionary new understanding of happiness and well-being. Simon and Schuster.

Fernández-Aráoz, C., Roscoe, A., & Aramaki, K. (2014). Turning potential into success: The missing link in leadership development. Harvard Business Review, 92(10), 86-93.

Garland, E. L., Hanley, A. W., Goldin, P. R., & Gross, J. J. (2015). Testing the mindfulness-to-meaning theory: Evidence for mindful positive emotion regulation from a reanalysis of longitudinal data. PloS one, 10(7), e0129864.

Huta, V., & Ryan, R. M. (2010). Pursuing pleasure or virtue: The differential and overlapping well-being benefits of hedonic and eudaimonic motives. Journal of Happiness Studies, 11(6), 735-762.

Luhmann, M., Hofmann, W., Eid, M., & Lucas, R. E. (2012). Subjective well-being and adaptation to life events: A meta-analysis. Journal of Personality and Social Psychology, 102(3), 592-615.

Berridge, K. C., & Kringelbach, M. L. (2015). Pleasure systems in the brain. Neuron, 86(3), 646-664.

Fredrickson, B. L. (2013). Positive emotions broaden and build. In Advances in experimental social psychology (Vol. 47, pp. 1-53). Academic Press.

Pressman, S. D., & Cohen, S. (2005). Does positive affect influence health?. Psychological bulletin, 131(6), 925-

971.
Waterman, A. S. (1993). Two conceptions of happiness: Contrasts of personal expressiveness (eudaimonia) and hedonic enjoyment. Journal of personality and social psychology, 64(4), 678-691.
Zinberg, N. E. (1984). Drug, set, and setting: The basis for controlled intoxicant use. Yale University Press.

ABOUT THE AUTHOR

Sachin J. Karnik possesses extensive experience and education in various domains within the social sciences, encompassing social work, addiction treatment, counseling, prevention, and related fields. Presently, he is collaborating with Angel Wing LLC in the creation and implementation of diverse programs designed to advance the organization's overarching mission. To acquire further details regarding the author's background and qualifications, kindly reach out to Angel Wing through the contact information provided at the commencement of this publication.